Mac

Beginners

The Complete and Easy Guide to Add Boho-Chic Charm to Your Modern Home and Garden with Plant Hangers, Wall Hanging, Homewares, and Other Stylish Projects

---

Molly Allen

Table of Contents

Introduction

Macramé is a form of textile clothing that involves not the typical method of weaving or knitting but by means of a chain of knots. It is believed that it started in the thirteenth century in the western hemisphere with Arab weavers. They tied excess strings and yarn at the ends of hand-woven fabrics for towels, scarves, and shawls on decorative ends.

Macramé Materials

Macramé stylists make use of different types of materials. The materials can be classified in two major ways; the natural materials and the synthetic materials.

Natural Materials

The qualities of natural materials differ from the synthetic material and knowing these qualities would help you to make better use of them. Natural cord materials existing today include Jute, Hemp, Leather, Cotton, Silk and Flax. There are also yarns made from natural fibers. Natural material fibers are made from plants and animals.

Synthetic Materials

Like natural materials, synthetic materials are also used in macramé projects. The fibers of synthetic materials are made through chemical processes. The major ones are nylon beading cord, olefin, satin cord and parachute cord.

Cord Measurement

Before you can embark on a macramé project, it is essential that you determine the amount of chord you will need. This includes knowing the length of the required cord and the total number of materials you have to purchase.

Equipment: to measure, you will need a paper for writing, pencil, tape rule and calculator. You would also need some basic knowledge of unit conversion as shared below:

- 1 inch = 25.4millimeters = 2.54 centimeters
- 1 foot =12 inches
- 1 yard = 3 feet = 36 inches
- 1 yard = 0.9 meters

Note: The circumference of a ring = 3.14 * diameter measured across the ring

Measuring Width

The first thing to do is determine the finished width of the widest area of your project. Once you have this width, pencil it down.

Next, determine the actual size of the materials, by measuring its width from edge to edge.

You can then proceed to determine the type of knot pattern you wish to use with the knowledge of the knot pattern. You must know the width and spacing (if required) of each knots. You should also determine if you want to add more cords to widen an area of if you would be needing extra cords for damps.

With the formula given above, calculate and determine the circumference of the ring of your designs.

Determine the mounting technique to be used. The cord can be mounted to a dowel, ring or other cord. Folded cords affect both the length and width of the cord measurement.

Cord Preparation

Though usually rarely emphasized, preparation of the cords and getting them ready for use in Macramé projects is one of the core pillars of the art of Macramé. At times, specialized processes such as conditioning and stiffening of cords need to be carried out before Macramé projects can be begun. In general, however, cord preparation in Macramé is mainly concerned with dealing with cut ends and preventing these ends from unraveling during the course of the project. During the course of a project, constant handing of materials can cause distortion in the ends which can end up having disastrous consequences on your project. Before starting your project, if you do not appropriately prepare special kinds of cords, like ones that were made by the twisting of individual strands, that cord is likely to completely come apart, effectively destroying your project.

Therefore, cord preparation is extremely and incomparably important to the success of any Macramé project, the preparation of each cord is meant to be done during the first step of making any knot, which is the step where you cut out your desired length of cord from the larger piece.

For cord conditioning, experts recommend rubbing beeswax along the length of the cord. To condition your cord, simply get a bit of beeswax, let it warm up a bit in your hands, and rub it along the cord's length. This will help prevent unwanted tight curls on your cord. Note that beeswax may be applied to both natural and synthetic materials. For synthetic materials however, only Satin and fine Nylon beading cords actually compulsorily require conditioning. After conditioning, inspect your cords for any imperfections and discard useless pieces to ensure the perfection of your project. After conditioning, then comes the actual process of cord preparation. Cords can be prepared (i.e. the ends can be prevented from fraying) through the use of a flame, a knot, tape and glue.

To prevent unraveling of your cord using a flame, firstly test a small piece of the material with the flame from a small lighter. The material needs to melt, not burn. If it burns, then such a cord is not suitable for flame preparation. To prepare using a flame, simply hold the cord to the tip of the flame for 2 to 5 seconds, make sure the cord does not ignite, but melts. Flame preparation is suitable for cords made from olefin, polyester and nylon, and the process is compulsory for the preparation of parachute cords.

Tying knots at the end of the cord is another effective method to prevent fraying. The overhand knot is an all-time favorite, but knots such as the figure 8 knot which is best suited to flexible cords can be used if you think the knot might have to be undone at some point of your project. The Stevedore knot can be used to prevent fraying when using slippery materials.

Glue is another priceless alternative that can be used to efficiently prevent fraying at the ends of cords. However, not all kinds of glue may be used in cord preparation. Only certain brands, such as the Aleen's Stop Fray may be used in cord preparation. Household glue might also be used, but only when diluted with water. TO prepare your cord, simply rub the glue on the ends of the material and leave it to dry. If you intend to pass beads over the glued end, roll the cord's end between your fingers to make it narrower as it dries. Nail polish may also be used as an alternative to glue.

Tape is also a reliable method to prepare your cords. Simply wrap the tape around the end of the cord where you want to prevent fraying of your material. Make sure the end of the cord remains narrow by squeezing it between your fingers. It is advisable to use masking tape or cellophane tape for your preparations.

A special class of Macramé cords, known as a parachute cord requires a special form of preparation. Parachute cords are composed of multiple core yarns surrounded by a braided sleeve. To prepare a parachute cord (also called a Paracord), pull out the core yarns from the sleeve, and expose the yarns by about half an inch. Now cut the core yarns back, so that they become even with the outer sleeve, and then push the sleeve forward till the yarns become invisible. To complete the preparation, apply flame to the outer sleeve till it melts, and then press the handle of your lighter onto the sleeve while it's still warm to flatten the area and keep it closed up. The melted area will look darker and more plastic than the rest of the material.

Finishing Techniques

Finishing techniques refer to the methods by which the ends of cords, after knots have been created may be taken care of to give a neat and tidy project. Finishing is often referred to as tying off. Several finishing knots are available, and are extremely effective methods for executing finishing processes. Reliable finishing knots include the overhand knot and the barrel knot, both of which are explained in detail in this book.

Folding techniques are also dependable finishing techniques. For flexible materials like cotton, all you need to do is fold the ends flat against the back surface and add glue to the ends to hold them in place. For less flexible materials, fold the cords to the back, then pass them under a loop from one or more knots, and then apply glue, allow it to dry, and cut off excess material.

Finally, you can do your finishing with the aid of fringes. You may choose between a brushed fringe and a beaded fringe.

Chapter 1: Macramé Patterns

Alternating Square Knots

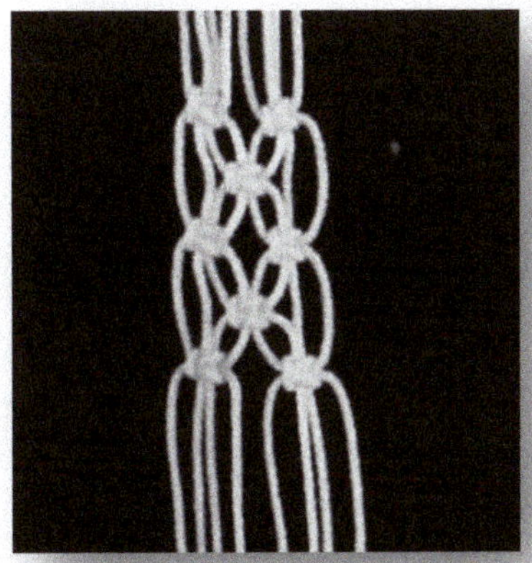

This is the perfect knot to use for basket hangings, decorations, or any projects that are going to require you to put weight on the project. Use a heavier weight cord for this, which you can find at craft stores or online.

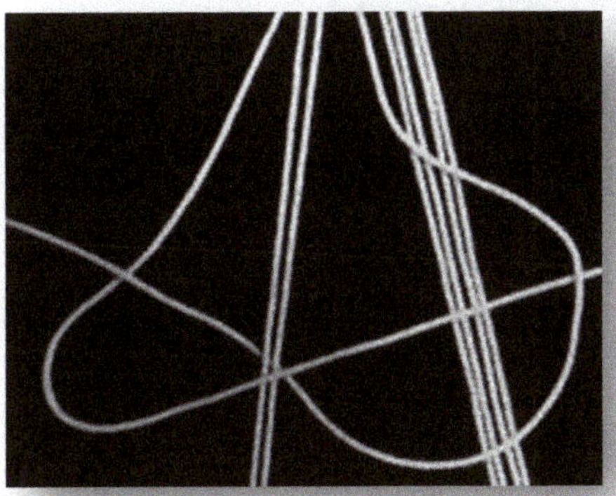

Watch the photos very carefully as you move along with this project and take your time to make sure you are using the right string at the right point of the project.

Don't rush, and make sure you have even tension throughout. Practice makes perfect, but with the illustrations to help you, you'll find it's not hard at all to create.

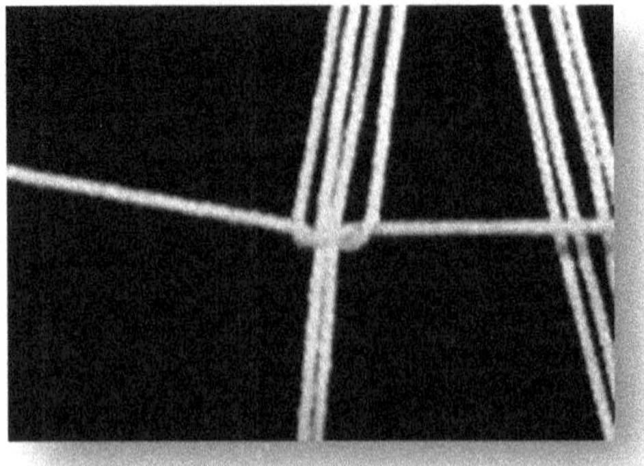

Start at the top of the project and work your way toward the bottom. Keep it even as you work your way throughout the piece. Tie the knots at 4-inch intervals, working your way down the entire thing.

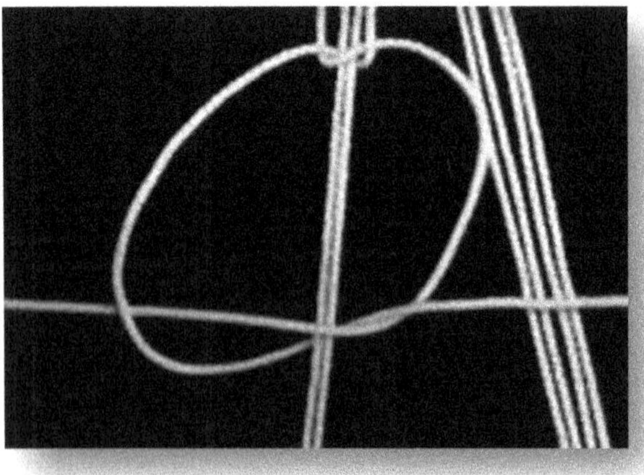

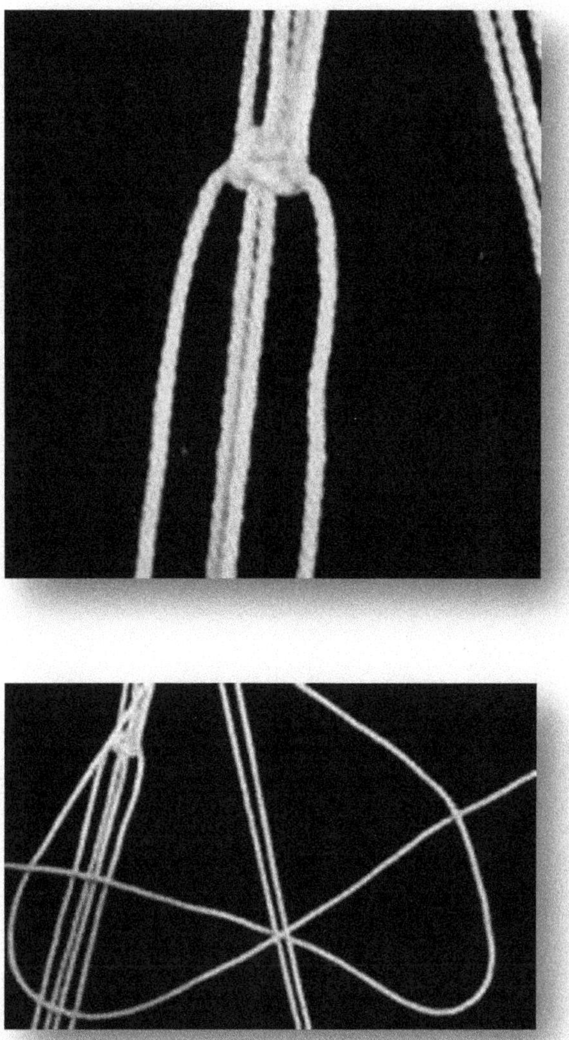

Tie each new knot securely. Remember that the more even you get the better it is.

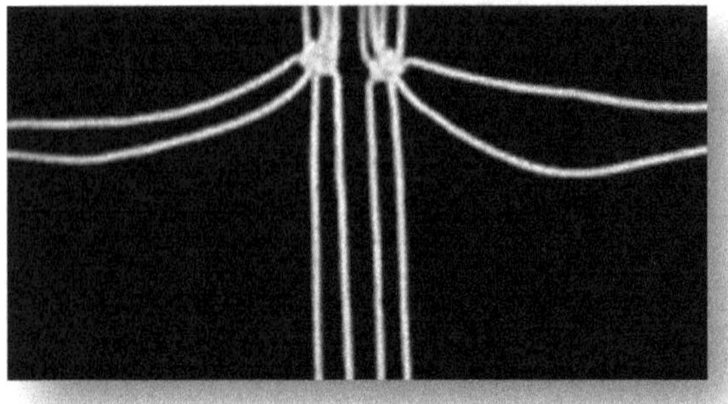

Work on one side of the piece first, then tie the knot on the other side. you are going to continue to alternate sides, with a knot joining them in the middle, as you can see in the photo
Again, keep this even as you work throughout.

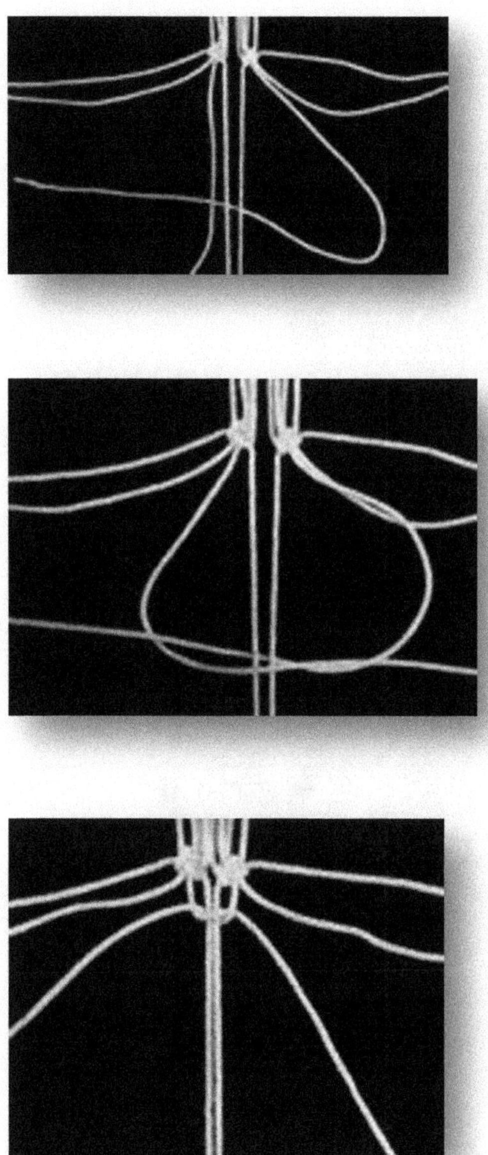

Bring the knot in toward the center and make sure you have even lengths on both sides of the piece.

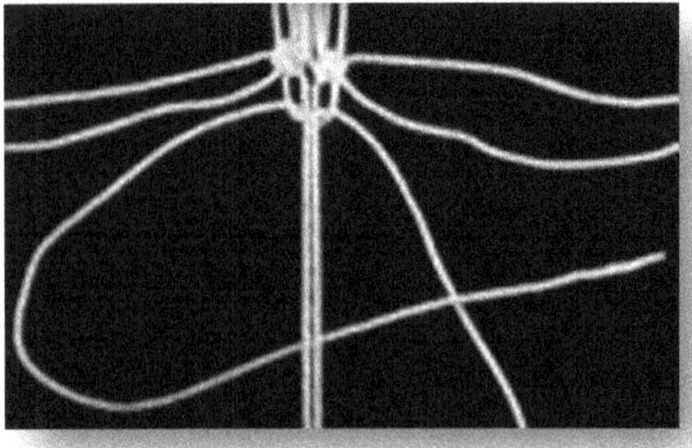

Pull this securely up to the center of the cord, then move on to the part on the cord.

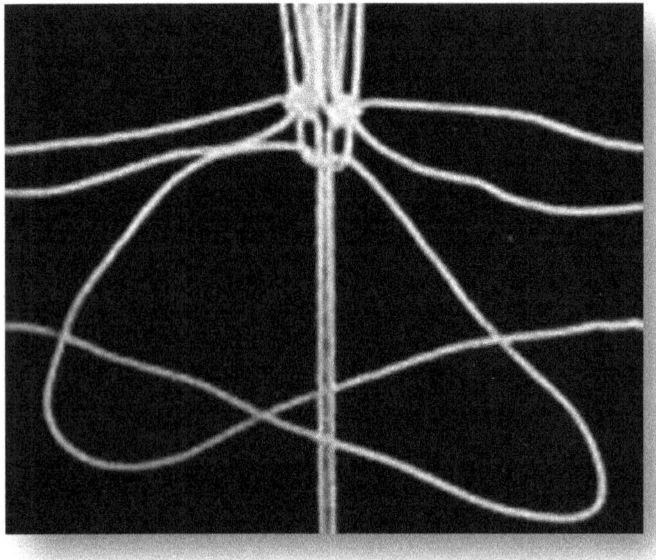

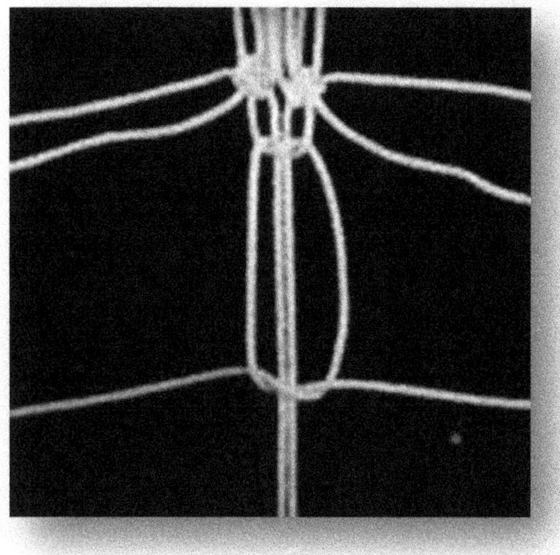

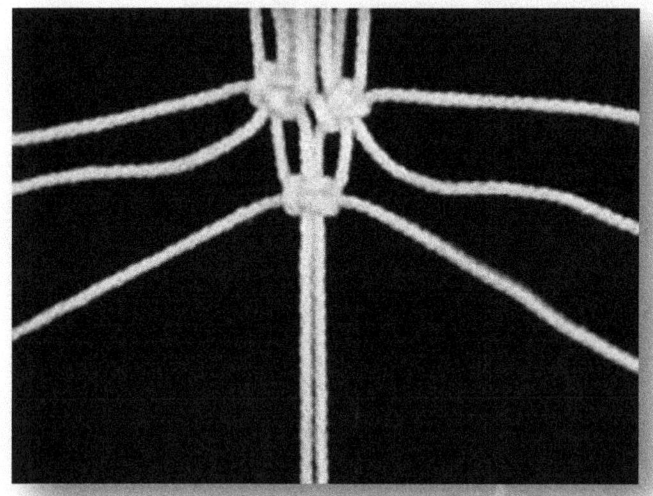

You are going to gather the cord on one side for the set of knots, and then you are going to go back to the other side of the piece to work another set of knots on the other side.

Work this evenly, then you are going to come back to the center.

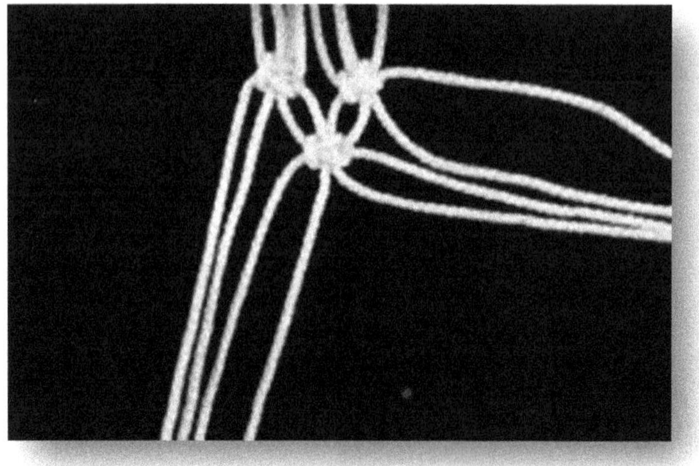

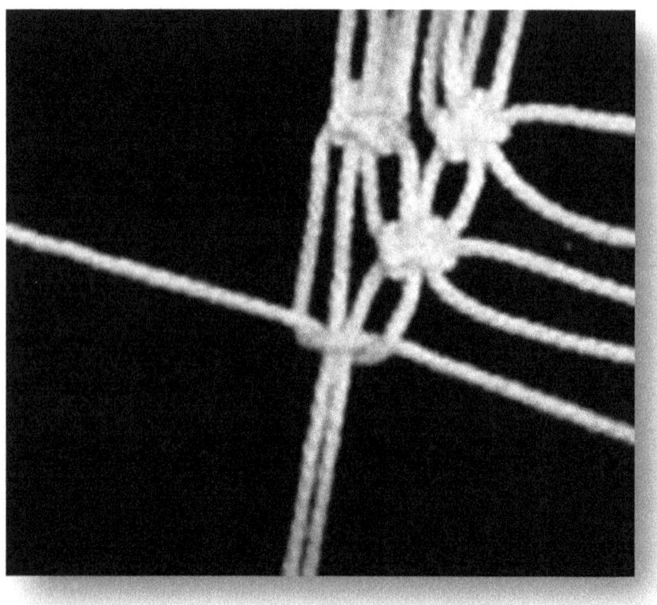

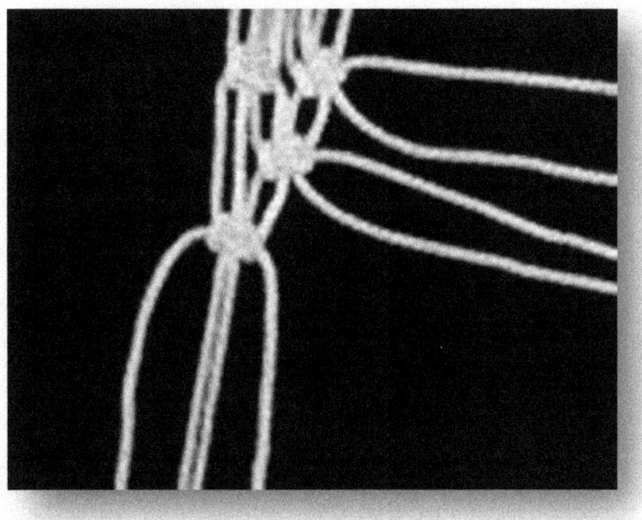

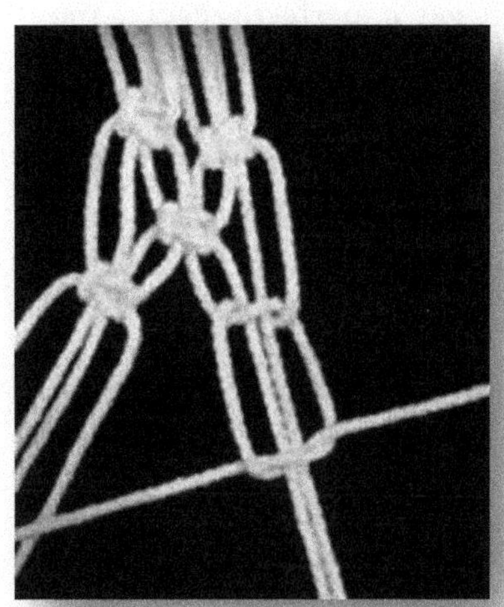

It's a matter of sequence. Work on the one side, then go back to the beginning, then go back to the other side once more. Continue to do this for as long as your cords are, or as long as you need for the project.

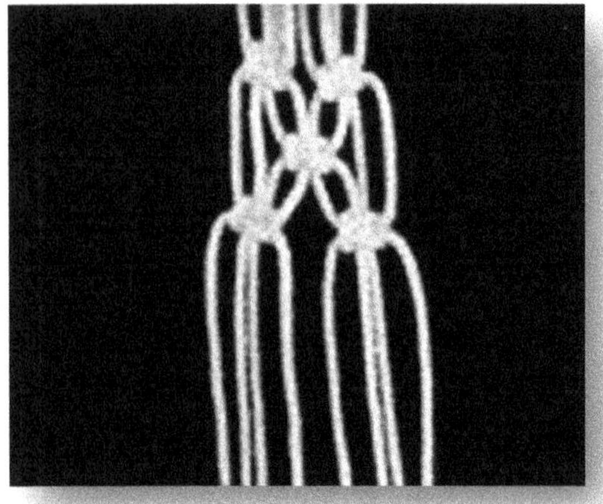

For the finished project, make sure that you have all your knots secure and firm throughout, and do your best to make sure it is all even. It is going to take practice before you can get it perfectly each time, but remember that practice does make perfect, and with time, you are going to get it without too much trouble.

Make sure all is even and secure and tie off. Snip off all the loose ends, and you are ready to go!

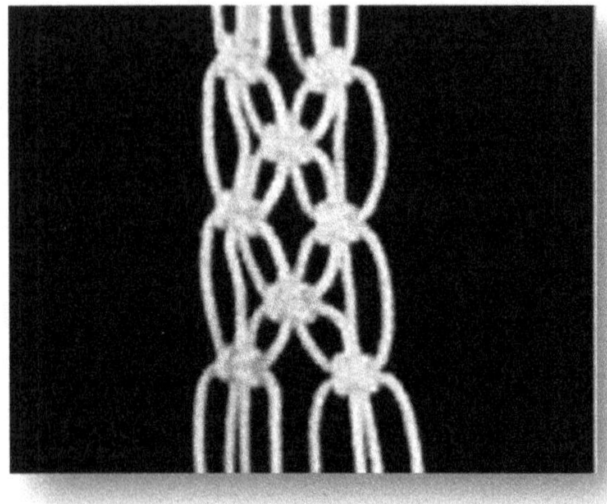

Capuchin Knot

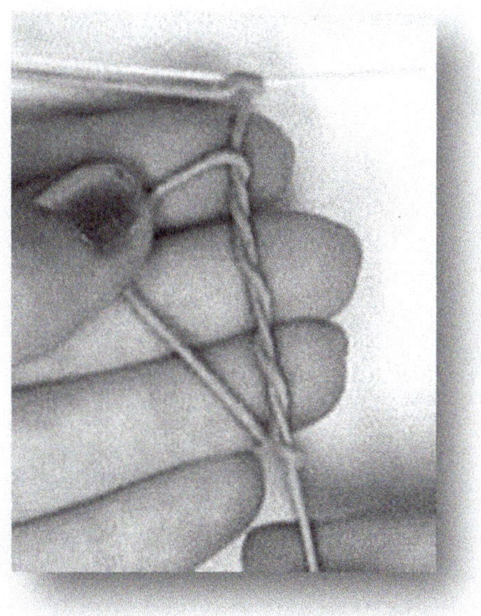

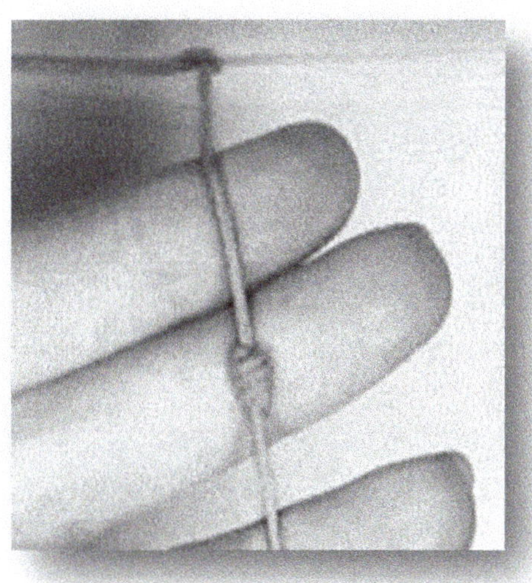

This is a great beginning knot for any project and can be used as the foundation for the base of the project. Use lightweight cord for this – it can be purchased at craft stores or online, wherever you get your macramé supplies.

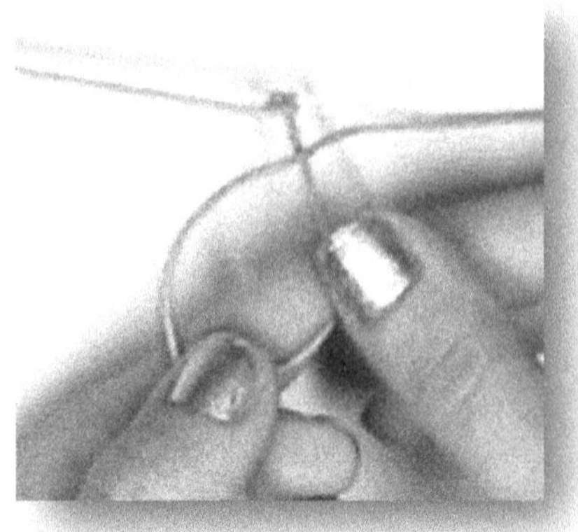

Watch the photos very carefully as you move along with this project and take your time to make sure you are using the right string at the right point of the project.

Don't rush, and make sure you have even tension throughout. Practice makes perfect, but with the illustrations to help you, you'll find it's not hard at all to create.

Start with the base cord, tying the knot onto this, and working your way along the project.

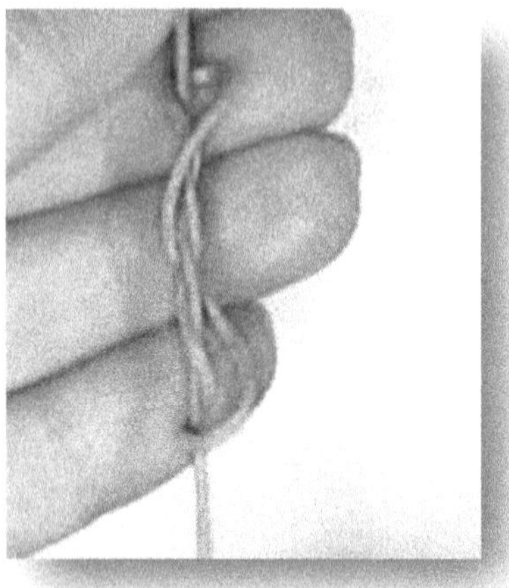

Twist the cord around itself 2 times, pulling the string through the center to form the knot.

For the finished project, make sure that you have all your knots secure and firm throughout, and do your best to make sure it is all even. It is going to take practice before you can get it perfectly each time, but remember that practice does make perfect, and with time, you are going to get it without too much trouble.

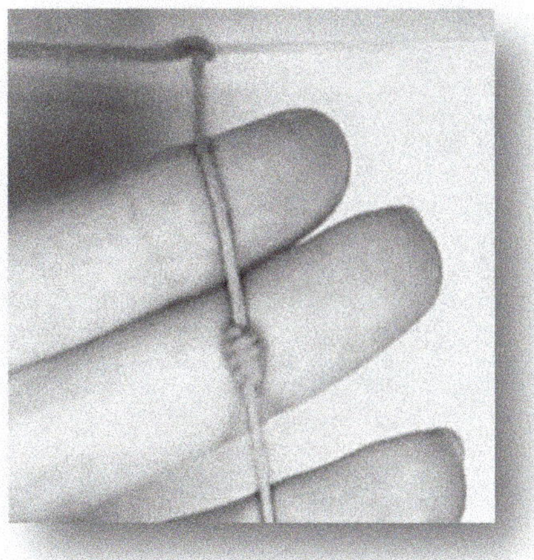

Make sure all is even and secure and tie off. Snip off all the loose ends, and you are ready to go!

Crown Knot

This is a great beginning knot for any project and can be used as the foundation for the base of the project. Use lightweight cord for this – it can be purchased at craft stores or online, wherever you get your macramé supplies.

Watch the photos very carefully as you move along with this project and take your time to make sure you are using the right string at the right point of the project.

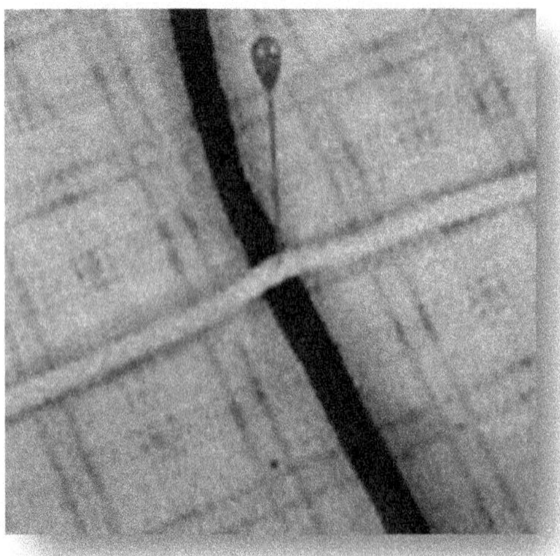

Don't rush, and make sure you have even tension throughout. Practice makes perfect, but with the illustrations to help you, you'll find it's not hard at all to create.

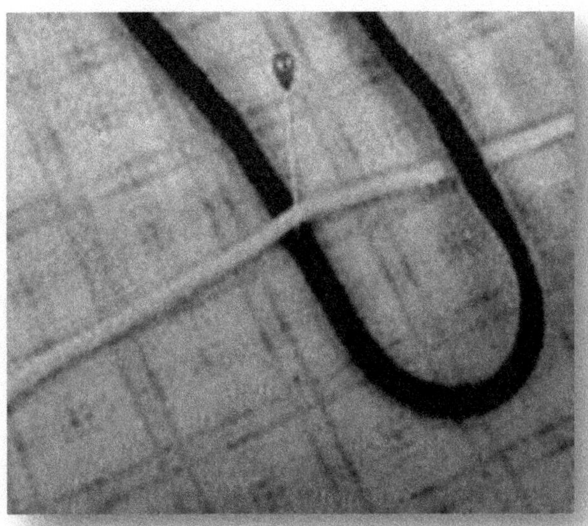

Use a pin to help keep everything in place as you are working.
Weave the strings in and out of each other as you can see in the photos. It helps to practice with different colors to help you see what is going on.

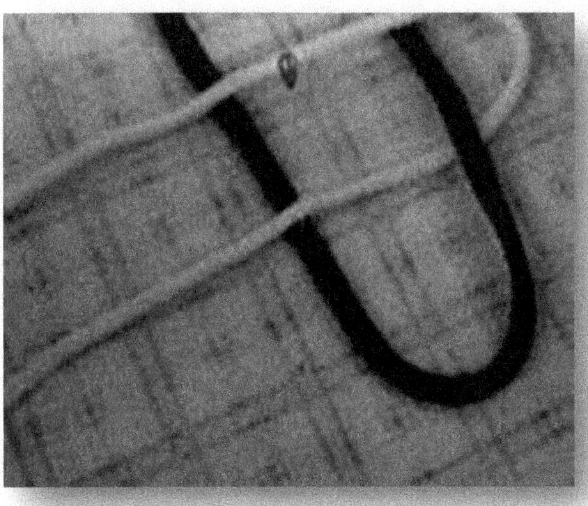

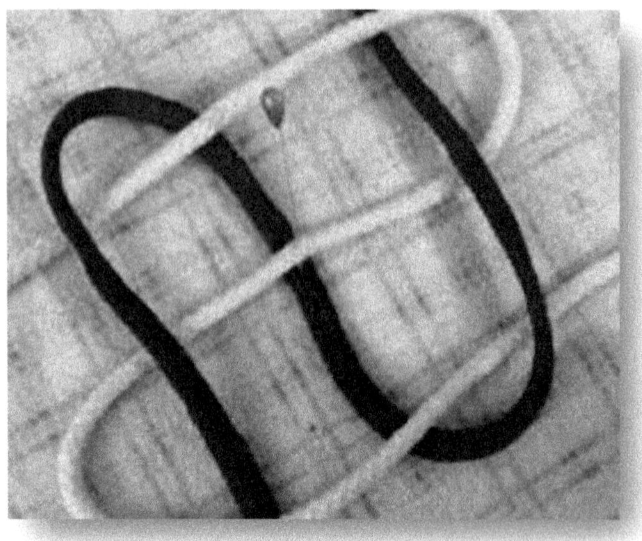

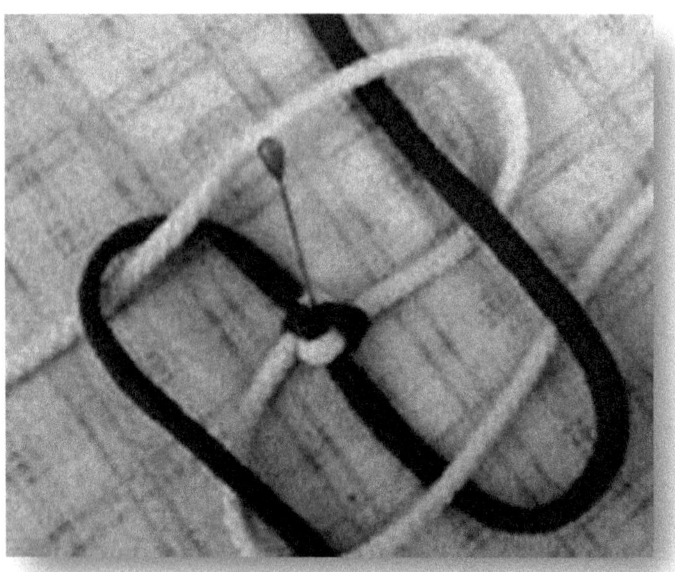

Pull the knot tight, and then repeat for the row on the outside.

Continue to do this as often as you like to create the knot. You can make it as thick as you like, depending on the project. You can also create more than one length on the same cord.

For the finished project, make sure that you have all your knots secure and firm throughout, and do your best to make sure it is all even. It is going to take practice before you can get it perfectly each time, but remember that practice does make perfect, and with time, you are going to get it without too much trouble.

Make sure all is even and secure and tie off. Snip off all the loose ends, and you are ready to go!

Diagonal Double Half Knot

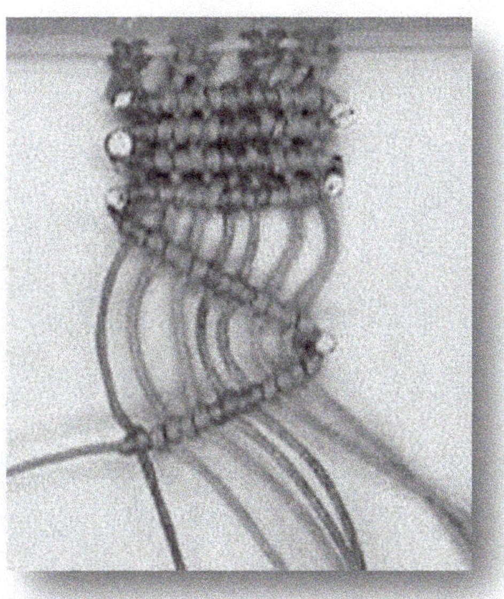

This is the perfect knot to use for basket hangings, decorations, or any projects that are going to require you to put weight on the project. Use a heavier weight cord for this, which you can find at craft stores or online.

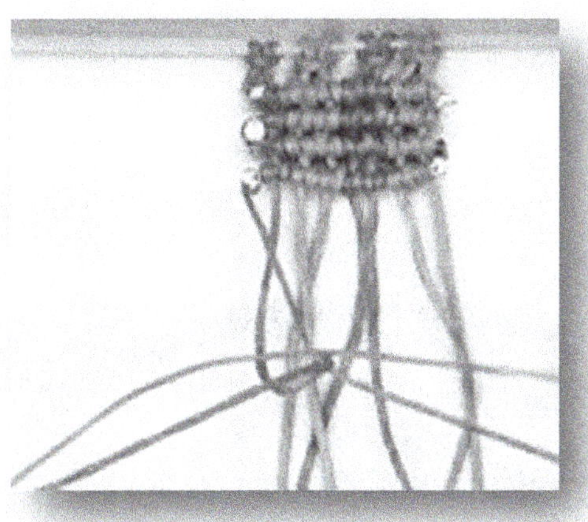

Watch the photos very carefully as you move along with this project and take your time to make sure you are using the right string at the right point of the project.

Don't rush, and make sure you have even tension throughout. Practice makes perfect, but with the illustrations to help you, you'll find it's not hard at all to create.

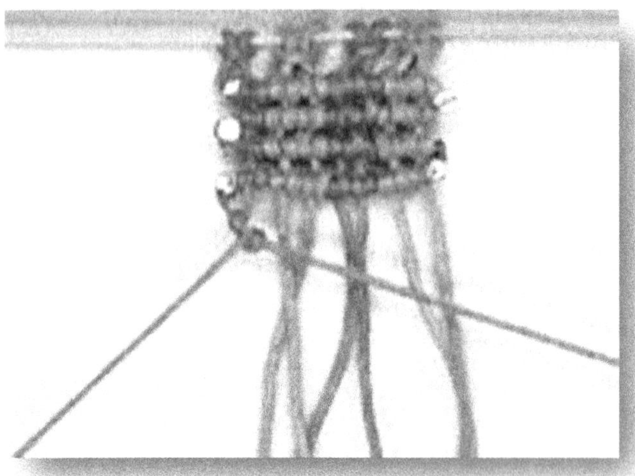

Start at the top of the project and work your way toward the bottom. Keep it even as you work your way throughout the piece. Tie the knots at 4-inch intervals, working your way down the entire thing.

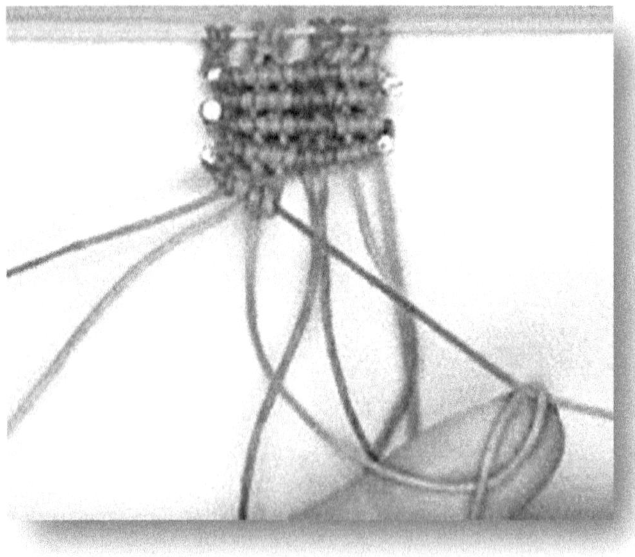

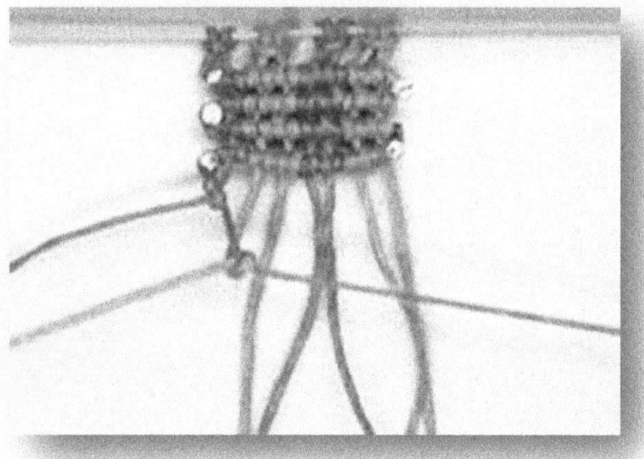

Weave in and out throughout, watching the photo as you can see for the right placement of the knots. Again, it helps to practice with different colors, so you can see what you need to do throughout the piece.

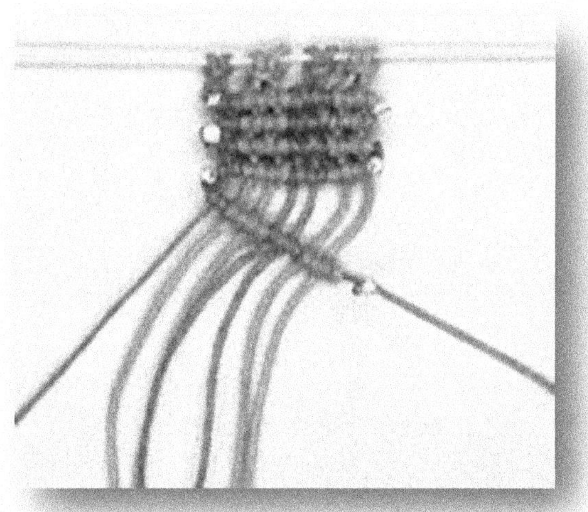

For the finished project, make sure that you have all your knots secure and firm throughout, and do your best to make sure it is all even. It is going to take practice before you can get it perfectly each time, but remember that practice does make perfect, and with time, you are going to get it without too much trouble.
Make sure all is even and secure and tie off. Snip off all the loose ends, and you are ready to go!

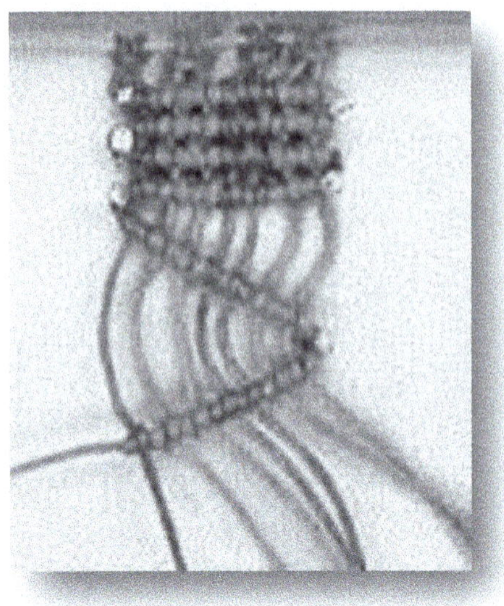

Frivolite Knot

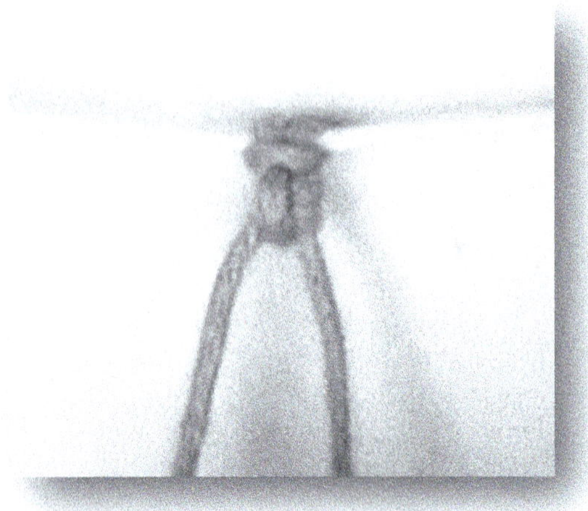

This is a great beginning knot for any project and can be used as the foundation for the base of the project. Use lightweight cord for this – it can be purchased at craft stores or online, wherever you get your macramé supplies.

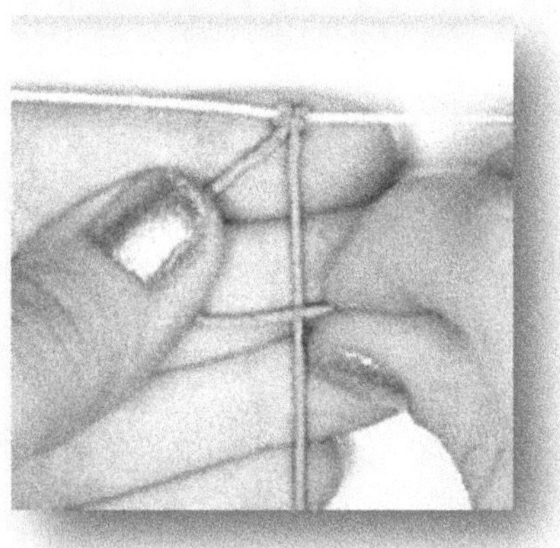

Watch the photos very carefully as you move along with this project and take your time to make sure you are using the right string at the right point of the project.

Don't rush, and make sure you have even tension throughout. Practice makes perfect, but with the illustrations to help you, you'll find it's not hard at all to create.

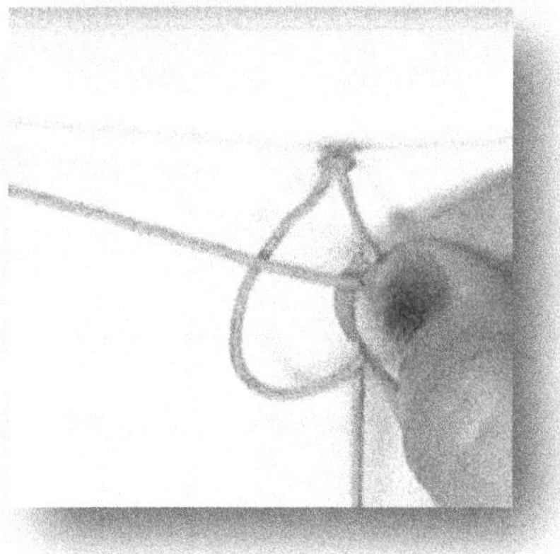

Use the base string as the guide to hold it in place, and then tie the knot onto this. This is a very straightforward knot; watch the photo and follow the directions you see.

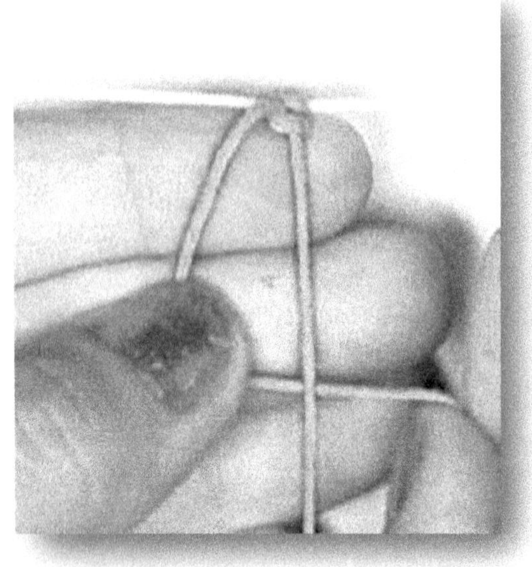

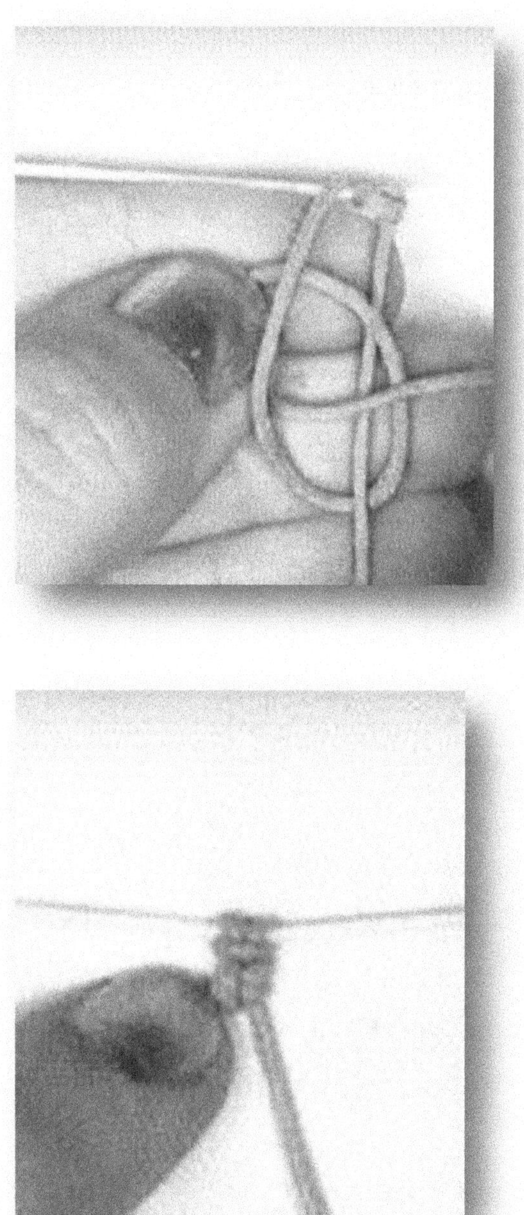

Pull the end of the cord up and through the center.

For the finished project, make sure that you have all your knots secure and firm throughout, and do your best to make sure it is all even. It is

going to take practice before you can get it perfectly each time, but remember that practice does make perfect, and with time, you are going to get it without too much trouble.
Make sure all is even and secure and tie off. Snip off all the loose ends, and you are ready to go!

Horizontal Double Half Knot

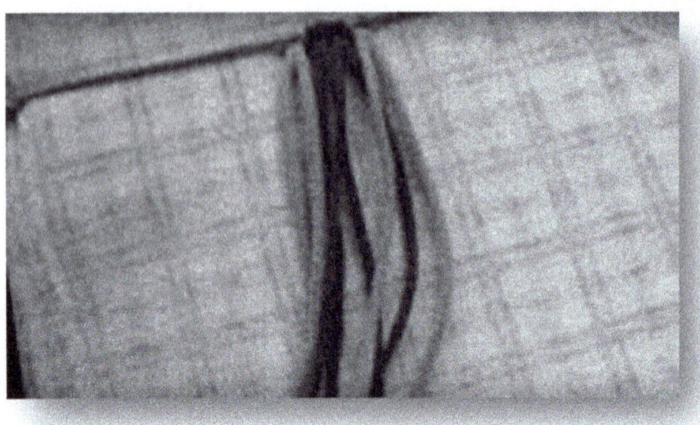

This is a great beginning knot for any project and can be used as the foundation for the base of the project. Use lightweight cord for this – it can be purchased at craft stores or online, wherever you get your macramé supplies.

Watch the photos very carefully as you move along with this project and take your time to make sure you are using the right string at the right point of the project.

Don't rush, and make sure you have even tension throughout. Practice makes perfect, but with the illustrations to help you, you'll find it's not hard at all to create.

Start at the top of the project and work your way toward the bottom. Keep it even as you work your way throughout the piece. Tie the knots

at 4-inch intervals, working your way down the entire thing.

For the finished project, make sure that you have all your knots secure and firm throughout, and do your best to make sure it is all even. It is going to take practice before you can get it perfectly each time, but remember that practice does make perfect, and with time, you are going to get it without too much trouble.

Make sure all is even and secure and tie off. Snip off all the loose ends, and you are ready to go!

Josephine Knot

This is the perfect knot to use for basket hangings, decorations, or any projects that are going to require you to put weight on the project. Use a heavier weight cord for this, which you can find at craft stores or online.

Watch the photos very carefully as you move along with this project and take your time to make sure you are using the right string at the right point of the project.

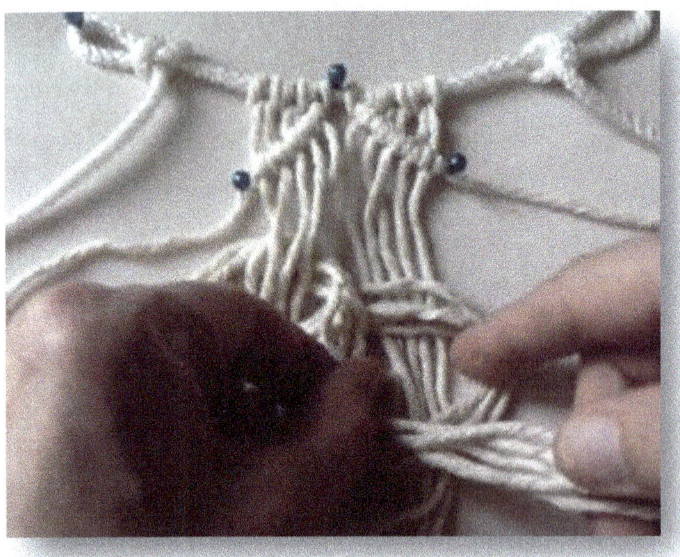

Don't rush, and make sure you have even tension throughout. Practice makes perfect, but with the illustrations to help you, you'll find it's not hard at all to create.

Use the pins along with the knots that you are tying, and work with larger areas all at the same time. This is going to help you keep the project in place as you continue to work throughout the piece.

Pull the ends of the knots through the loops and form the ring in the center of the strings.

For the finished project, make sure that you have all your knots secure and firm throughout, and do your best to make sure it is all even. It is going to take practice before you can get it perfectly each time, but remember that practice does make perfect, and with time, you are going to get it without too much trouble.

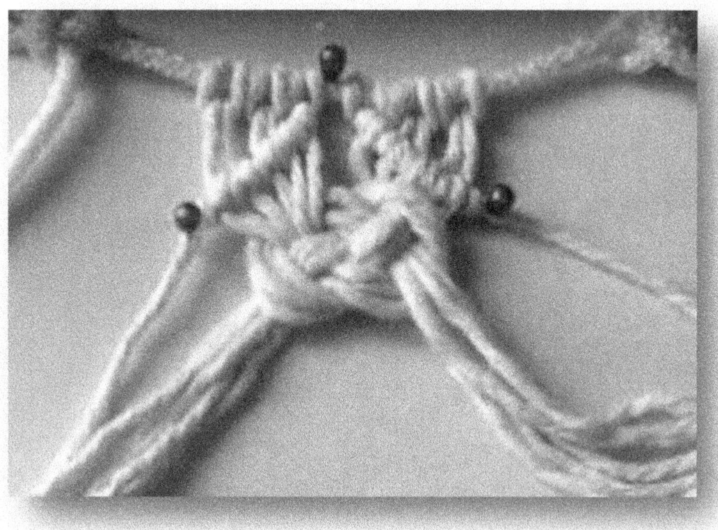

Make sure all is even and secure and tie off. Snip off all the loose ends, and you are ready to go!

Chapter 2: Projects

DIY Macramé Feathers

Beautiful, wispy macramé feathers clogged my social media pages as late as possible but I'm not crazy about it. They are incredibly beautiful, and I certainly got to buy them so I had to bookmark, to hang in the room of the children. But I was also curious about how they were made, of course. How do you achieve this perfectly soft fringe in the world? It involves a brush of a cat. Enough has been said. Honestly though, there are endless possibilities here, and I could not wait to play more with this technique. But I hope I'll inspire you to do these at home in the meantime.

Cut for a medium-sized feather:

- 1 32" strands around the spine
- 10-12 14" strands around the top
- 8-10 12" strands around the middle
- 6-8 10" strands around the bottom

Fold in half the 32 "strand. Choose one of the 14", fold them in half and tuck them under the spine. Take the next 14 "strand, fold it in half and attach it into the top horizontal strand loop. Pull this through and lay it horizontally on top of the oppositional strand. Now pull the bottom strands through the top loop all the way. Pull both ends of the spectrum tightly. In the next row, you will alternate the starting side. Pull through the top loop the lower threads. And squeeze. Keep going and work in scale slowly.

Push up the strands to tighten-grab the lower end of the middle strand (spine) with one hand and push up the strands with the other. Once finished, drag the fringe down to meet the middle strand's bottom. Give her a rough trim instead. Not only does this help guide the shape, but it also helps to brush out the strands. To be honest, the shorter the lines, the better. It also helps to have a very sharp tissue shear pair!

Start at the spine when brushing and push hard when brushing into the thread. To get that perfect, delicate fringe, it will take many hard strokes. Work down your way. Do not want the brush to throw off any strands while you brush the lower end of the spinal cord. You're going to want to stiffen the feather next. The cords are soft that it is just flopping if you collect it and try to hang it. Give it a spray, or two, and allow at least a few hours to be tried.

DIY Tassel and Macramé Key chains

Who doesn't love a sweet ring? Particularly a lovely DIY version which takes no time to make, uses stuff you've already got, can be as simple or as fantastic as you want? If you need an excuse to make a personalized keychain, we have you:

Update your keychain before remembering it, create a replacement set of keys for your domestic pet sitter, make a replacement set of keys you can leave from your neighbor so that when you lockout you have not to break into your place.

Organize yourself by making a special key ring for all those small rewards cards. Use this to improve your macramé skills. For the stripped Macramé keychain, I used vertical clove hitch knots and wool-roving thread. The third and fifth personalized keychain is super easy – strings and a few Perles with a tassel. And the fourth DIY keychain is only a long braid, folded in half, wrapped in floss of embroidery. Beads are hand-painted and made from Sculpey.

Materials needed for Macramé Key chains

- Key Ring
- 3/16" Natural Cotton Piping Cord
- Beads
- Embroidery yarn or floss
- Scissors

You can make things fancy on your key chains tassel or macramé by wrapping them in different yarn or floss colors.

Macramé Curtain

Tie four strands together on the same foam core board and place pins in the top knot to keep those in place beneath the two center strands. Take the right outer strand (pink) and pass it over the other two center fibers to the left side. Take the left (yellow) outer strand and pass it under the pink strand that is behind the middle fibers and on the other side over the pink strand. Push closely the two strands. Then, in the first step, you just reverse what you did! Take the leftmost strand (now the pink) and lay it over two strands in the middle. Take the extreme right strand (which is now the yellow) and transfer it under the pink, behind the two middle strands, and on the other side over the pink. Pull the two strands tightly until they create a knot from the woven strands. That's the most difficult part! These basic motions are repeated by the rest of the steps. To make another knot right next to your first knot, repeat steps 1-3 with four more threads. Put in two right strands of the first knot for a new group with two leftmost strands of the second knot.

Repeat with the new group your basic knot by taking the outer right (purple) strand and passing it over the middle two strands to the left side. Take the outside (green) left and pass it through the purple strand, after the medium strands, and across the purple strand on the other side. Push closely the two fibers. Now turn the first step back! Take the leftmost strand (which is the purple now) and lay it over two strands in the middle. Take the extreme right strand (the green) and pass it under the purple, behind the two middle strands, and across the violet on the other side. Pull closely these two threads. By moving the two leftmost threads and the two rightmost strands, divide the middle group of strands. Repeat the fundamental knot with both classes and continue until so long as you like.

I built 14 rope classes, each with four lines, all 100 inches long when I began the actual curtain. It made a clean knot to cut two cords twice as long (thus 200 inches) on top of the curtain and then hung strands across the rod at the middle point and tied up a knot to create a group of four strands. Since doing this method with big ropes is much larger than the thread, you're going to have to find something to hang your rod from so you let your rope hang under it (we've used a bike rack to hang our rope).

You can see that making the simple knots with the yarn is the same idea, but only on a much larger scale. I rendered the base knot near the top of all 14 bands and then made a new knot line below and above them (as in the yarn instructions). I then went down a new row, took knots under the original knots, and kept the knots rowing until I had finished all the rows I needed. Make sure you stay back while you make your knots to make sure you tie your knots in even rows. I maintained a handy ruler so that. I dropped the rest of the strands to complete the curtain until 5 rows of knots were completed.

Hang your new curtain in your perfect place once you have finished braiding the ropes. Finally, wrap the masking cassette at the ends where the cloth reaches the ground, which is 6 1/2 feet tall (or white cassette which is "dorm cassette') I have used. Slice the candle and leave intact 2/3 to half of the candle. It helps to prevent spawning of overtime. I hung an off-white piece of textile on the macramé curtain (on the existing clothes rack). I love how it turned out that curtain! It feels different but still functional, not too loud. We've got a very loud rug in the room so we didn't need anything with tons of color or a lot of attention.

Wall Hanging

Materials

To make this wall hanging you will need the following materials:

- 18x 5 meter (16, 5 foot) of 5mm (0, 2") cotton rope
- 7x 50cm (20") of 5mm cotton rope
- 1x A wood dowel 44cm (17") long

Starting your wall hanging

To start your wall hanging cut 18 sections of cotton rope 5 meters (16,5 foot) each. You will need to attach all 18 ropes using a Lark's head knot. To make this knot take 1 rope and fold it in half. Pull the folded end over the wood dowel and pull the cord ends through the loop you just made. Repeat this step 18 times.

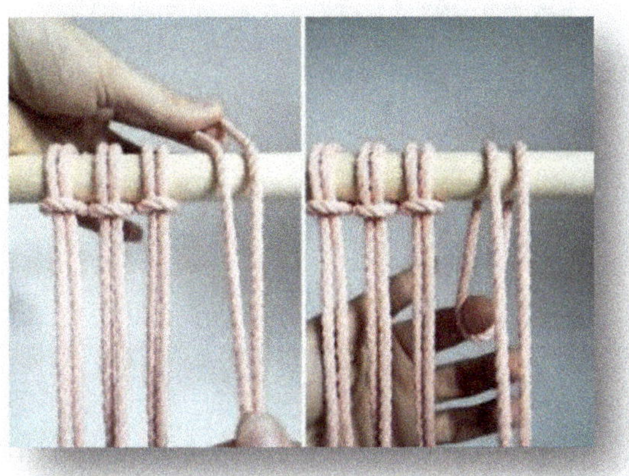

Now it is time for the first horizontal line of double half-hitch knots. First use 1 of your 50cm (20") cotton rope to use as you holding cord. Now use your hanging cords to tie 36 double half-hitch knots around your holding cord.

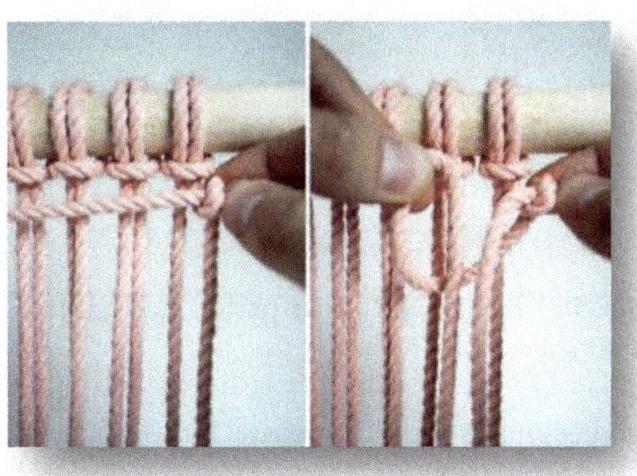

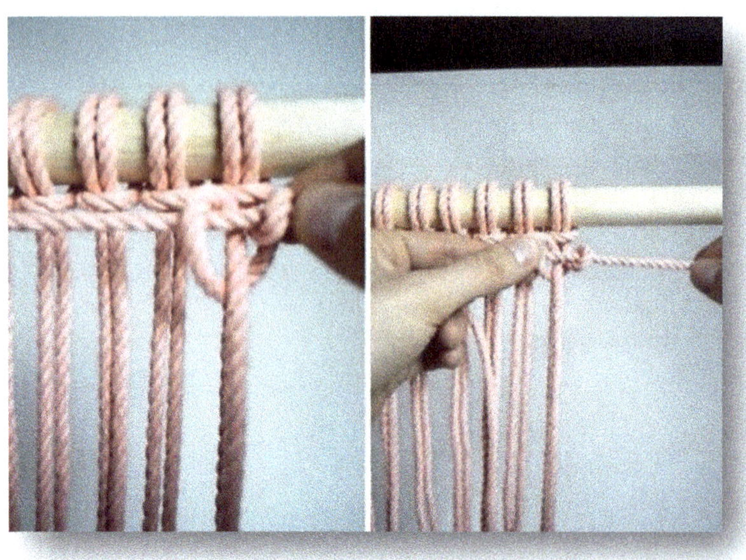

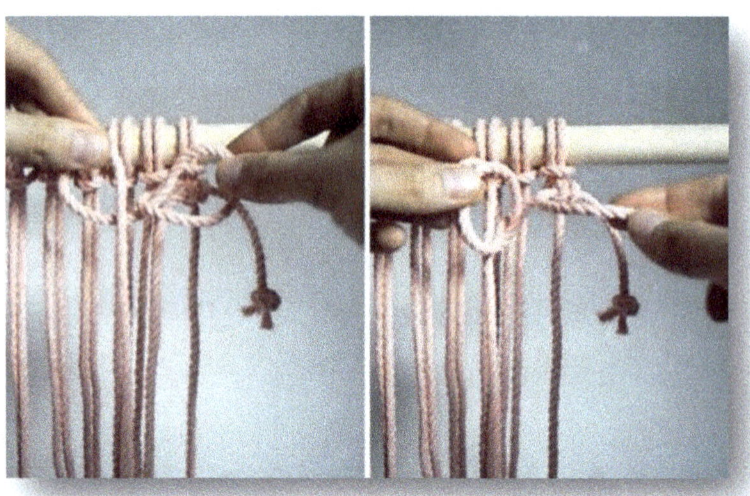

The 4 patterns

The wall hanging consists of 4 distinct different patterns. Each pattern is locked in by 2 horizontal rows of half-hitch knots.

The honeycomb pattern

The first part of this wall hanging is the easiest part. First you start out with a row of square knots. Next a row of 2 square knots followed by a row of single square knots. Repeat this once more. To finish the first part tie a horizontal row of half-hitch knots. Leave a small gap of about 2.5cm (1") and tie another horizontal row of half-hitch knots.

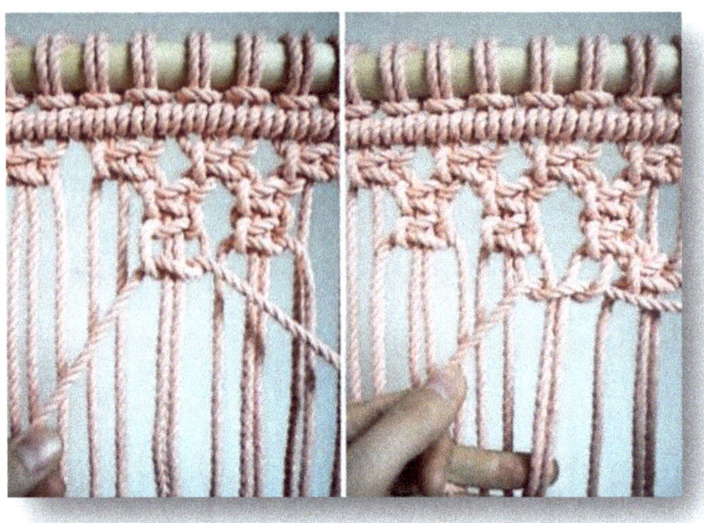

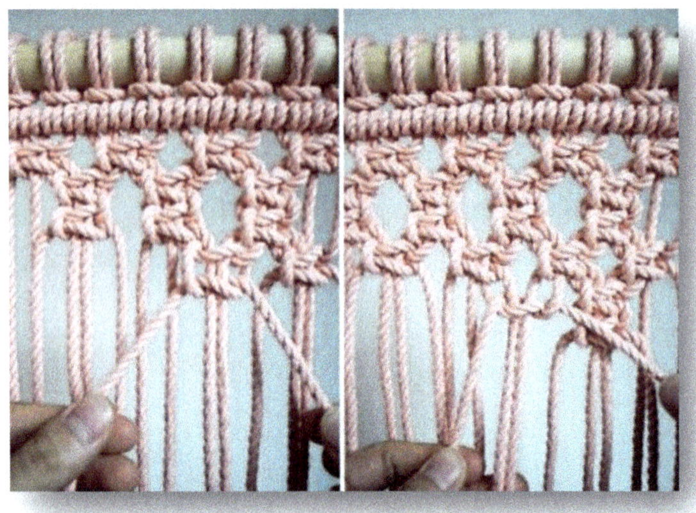

Half-hitch crosses

Each cross uses 8 cords. In total this wall hanging has 36 cords. We need to leave 2 cords untouched on both sides of the wall hangings. So we start out with the 3rd cord as our holding cord. Tie double half-hitch knots diagonally around this holding cord with cord 4, 5 and 6. Use cord 10 as your holding cord and tie double half-hitch knots diagonally around this cord with cord 9, 8 and 7. Now use your left holding cord to tie a double half hitch around the right holding cord. Continue to tie diagonal half-hitch knots with cord 6, 5 and 4 and 7, 8 and 9. Repeat this entire step 3 more times for the remaining 3 crosses.

Once you have finished all 4 crosses it is time to make another horizontal row of double half-hitch knots.

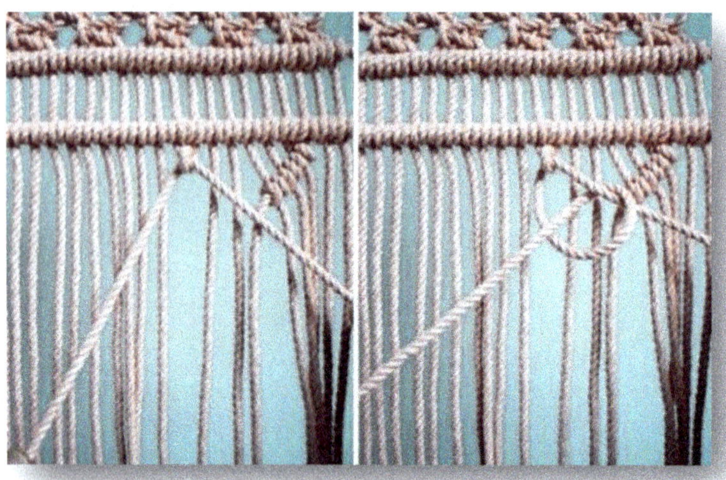

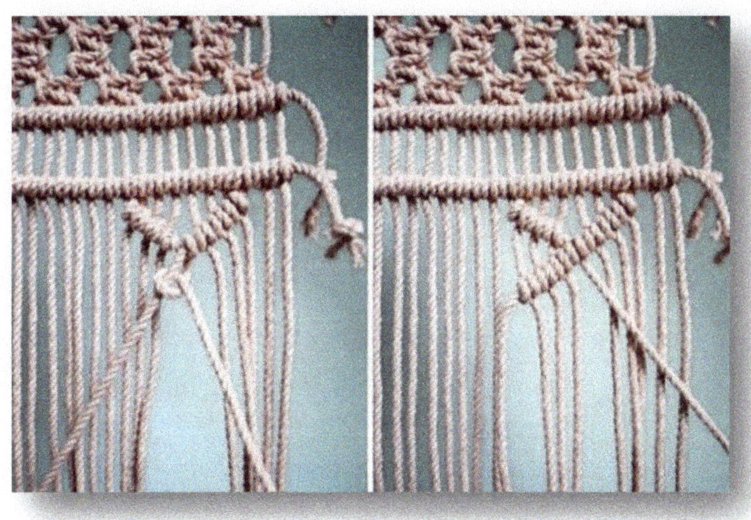

Half square knots

For this part we will be using only the first half of the square knot. In total tie 5 rows of half square knots. Leave about 2cm (0, 8") between each row. Finish this part with another horizontal row of double half-hitch knots.

Square knots and half-hitch knots

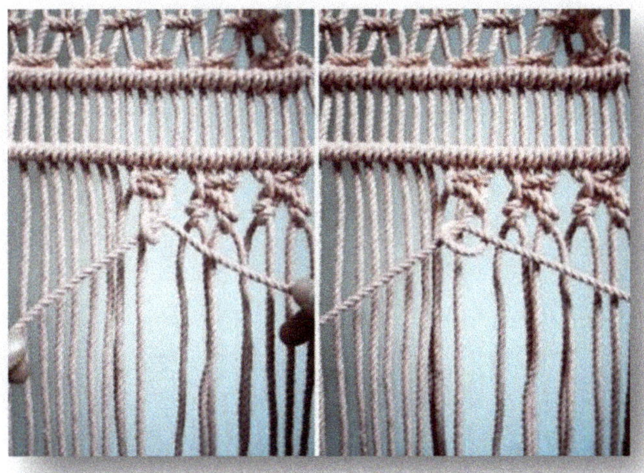

This is the most complex part of the wall hanging. We will be using a combination of square knots and half-hitch knots. First start with a row of square knots. Now each square knot has 4 cords hanging down. Use the outside cord as your holding cord and use the inside cord as your working cord to tie 1 diagonal double half-hitch knot. Repeat this for all cords. Tie a row of square knots followed by another row of the diagonal half-hitch knots. Finish the pattern with 1 last row of square knots followed by the last horizontal row of double half-hitch knots.

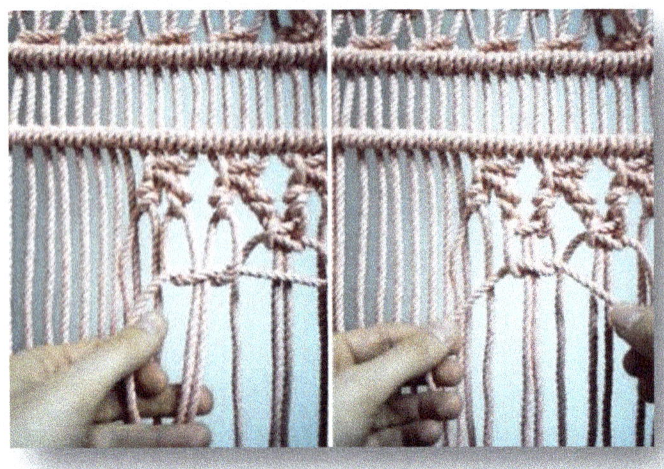

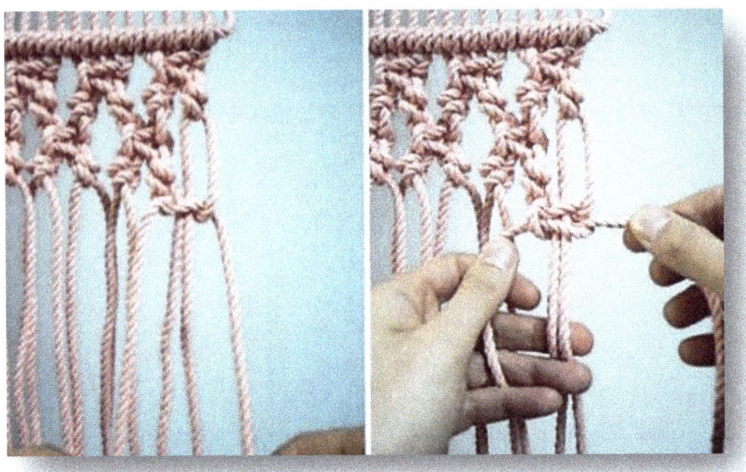

Weaving the loose ends and cutting the fringe

Your wall hanging is now almost done. Just the finishing touches are left. First it is time to weave in the loose ends of the holding cords of the horizontal rows. Lay your wall hanging flat on the floor upside down. Use a scissor to loosen the back of one of double half-hitch knots and pull the loose end through. Cut the end. If you wish to prevent any fraying you can use some tape on the ends. Once you finished all loose ends it is time to hang your wall hanging and trim the fringe. If you wish you can untie and brush out the fringe to create a fluffier look.

Chapter 3: Plant Hanger

Macramé Plant Hanger Beginner

Description: Plant hanger of 2 feet and 5.5 inches (75 cm)
Knots: Square knot, alternating square knot, half knot and gathering knot.
Supplies:

- Cord: 10 strands of cord of 18 feet and 0.5 inches (5, 5 meter), 2 strands of 3 feet and 3.3 inches (1 meter)
- Ring: 1 round ring (wood) of 1.6 inches (4 cm) diameter
- Container: 7 inches (18 cm) diameter

Directions (step-by-step):

1. Fold the 10 long strands of cord in half through the wooden ring.

2. Tie all (now 20) strands together with 1 shorter strand with a gathering knot. Hide the cut cord ends after tying the gathering knot.
3. Make a square knot using all cords: use from each side 4 strands to make the square knot; the other 12 strands stay in the middle.
4. Divide the strands in 2 sets of 10 strands each. Tie a square knot in each set using 3 strands on each side (4 strands stay in the middle of each group).
5. Divide the strands in 3 sets of 6 strands for the outer groups and 8 strands for the group in the middle. Tie a square knot in each set using 2 strands on each side.
6. Divide the strands into 5 sets of 4 strands each and make a square knot with each set.
7. Continue with the 5 sets. In the 2 outer sets you tie 4 square knots and in the 3 inner sets, you tie 9 half knots.

8. Using all sets tie 7 alternating square knots by connecting two strands in each set with the right two strands of the set to it. In the first, third, fifth and seventh row you are not using the 2 outer strands on each side.
9. Repeat step 7 and 8. In repeating step 8 you tie 5 alternating square knots instead of 7 alternating square knots.
10. To help you with the steps, number the strands from left to right, numbering them no.1 to no. 20.

11. With the 4 middle strands (no. 9 tot 12) you make 14 square knots.
12. Make a square knot with the set of 4 strands no. 3 to 6 and the set of 4 strands no. 15 to 18.

13. Divide the strands into 4 sets of 4 strands (ignore the set with the 14 square knots in the middle) and tie 12 square knots in each set.
14. Drop down 2 inches (5 cm).

15. Make 5 sets in the following way and tie in each set a square knot:

- Set 1 consists out of strands no. 5, 6, 1 and 2
- Set 2 consists out of strands no. 3, 4, 9 and 10
- Set 3 consists out of strands no. 7, 7, 13 and 14
- Set 4 consists out of strands no. 11, 12, 17 and 18
- Set 5 consists out of strands no. 19, 20, 16 and 15

16. Drop down another 2 inches (5 cm), no knots. This is the moment to place your chosen container/bowl into the hanger to make sure it will fit. If you need to leave more space without knots in order to fit your container, you can do so.

17. Gather all strands together and then tie a gathering knot with the left-over shorter strand. Trim all strands at different lengths to finish your project.

Macramé Plant Hanger Intermediate

Description: Plant hanger of 4 feet and 3 inches (1, 30 meter)
Knots: Square knot, alternating square knot, half knot, alternating half hitch, gathering knot.
Supplies:

- Cord: 8 strands of cords of each 26 feet and 3 inches (8 meter), 1 short strand of cord
- Wooden Ring: 1 round ring (wood) of 1, 6 inches (4 cm) diameter
- Container/Flowerpot: 7 inches (18 cm) diameter

Directions (step-by-step):

1. Fold 8 strands of cord, the long ones, in half over and through the ring. Now you have 16 strands of cord in total. Group them in sets of four strands.
2. Tie 4 square knots on each set of four strands.

3. Drop down 3.15 inches (8 cm).
4. Tie 4 strands in each set with the right two of the set to it. Repeat on each of the 4 sets.
5. Drop down 4.3 inches (11 cm).
6. Repeat step 4, starting with the 2 right strands this time.

7. Take 2 strands of 1 set and make 10 alternating half hitch knots. Repeat for the 2 left strands of that set. Repeat for all sets.

8. Drop down 3.9 inches (10 cm) and tie a row of 48 half knots on each set of four strands.

9. Take the 2 middle strands of each set and make 8 alternating half hitch knots. You leave the 2 strands on the side of the set as they are (without knots).
10. Tie a row of 30 half knots on each set of four strands.

11. Use a new short strand of cord to make a gathering knot around all strands.
12. Cut off and fray the ends as desired.

Macramé Plant Hanger Advanced

Description: Plant hanger of 2 feet and 5.5 inches (75 cm)
Knots: Square knot,alternating square knot, crown knot, gathering knot and overhand knot.
Supplies:

- Cord: 4 strands of cord of 13 feet and 1.5 inches (4 meter), 4 strands of 16 feet and 4.8 inches (5 meter), 2 strands of 3 feet and 3.4 inches (1 meter)
- Ring: 1 round ring (wood) of 1.5 inches (4 cm) diameter
- Beads: wooden beads
- Cristal Bowl/Container: 7 inches (18 cm) diameter

Directions (step-by-step):

1. Fold the 8 long strands of cord (4 strands of 13 feet and 1.5 inches and 4 strands of 16 feet and 4.8 inches) in half through the wooden ring.
2. Tie all (now 16) strands together with 1 shorter strand with a gathering knot. Hide the cut cord ends after tying the gathering knot.

3. Divide the strands into 4 sets of 4 strands each. Each set has 2 long strands and 2 shorter strands. Tie 5 Chinese crown knots in each set. Pull each strand tight and smooth.

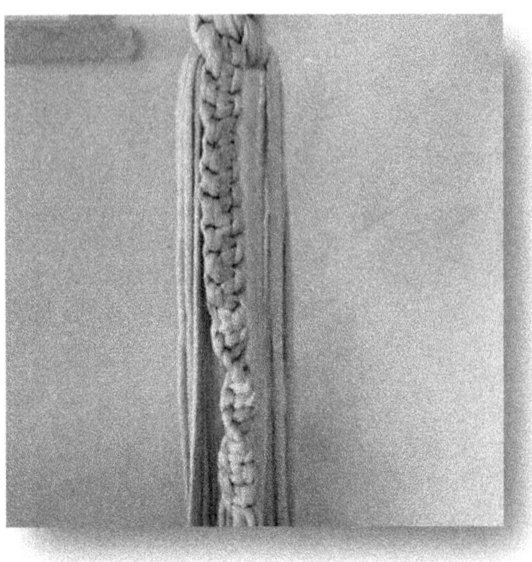

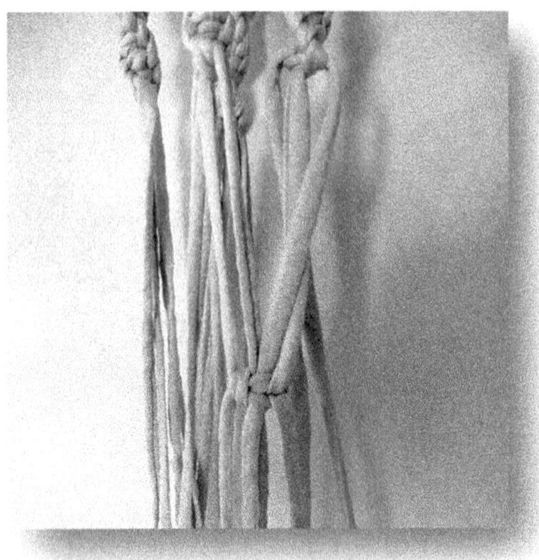

4. Tie 8 square knots on each set of four strands. In each set the 2 shorter strands are in the middle and you are tying with the 2 outer, longer strands.
5. Tie 15 half square knots with each set.

6. Drop down 5.5 inches (14 cm), no knots, and tie an alternating square knot to connect the left two cords in each set to it.
7. Drop down 3.15 inches (8 cm) and tie again an alternating square knot with 4 strands.

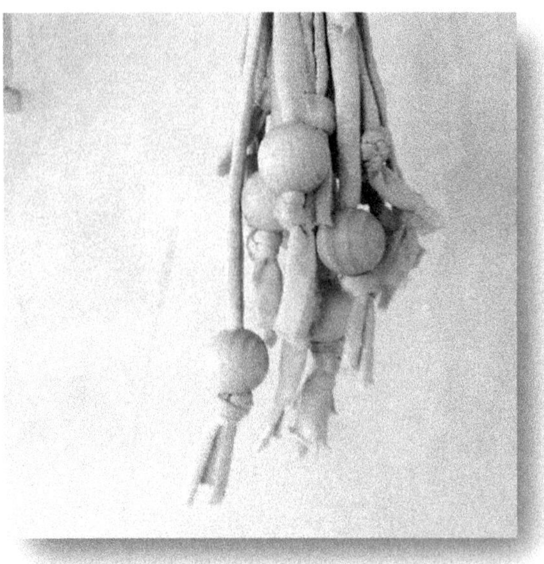

8. Drop down 1.5 inches (4 cm). Place your chosen container/bowl into the hanger to make sure it will fit, gather all strands together and then tie a gathering knot with the left-over shorter strand. Add a bead to each strand end (optional). Tie an overhand knot in each strand and trim all strands just below the overhand knots.

Chapter 4: Macramé Jewelry

Hoop Earrings

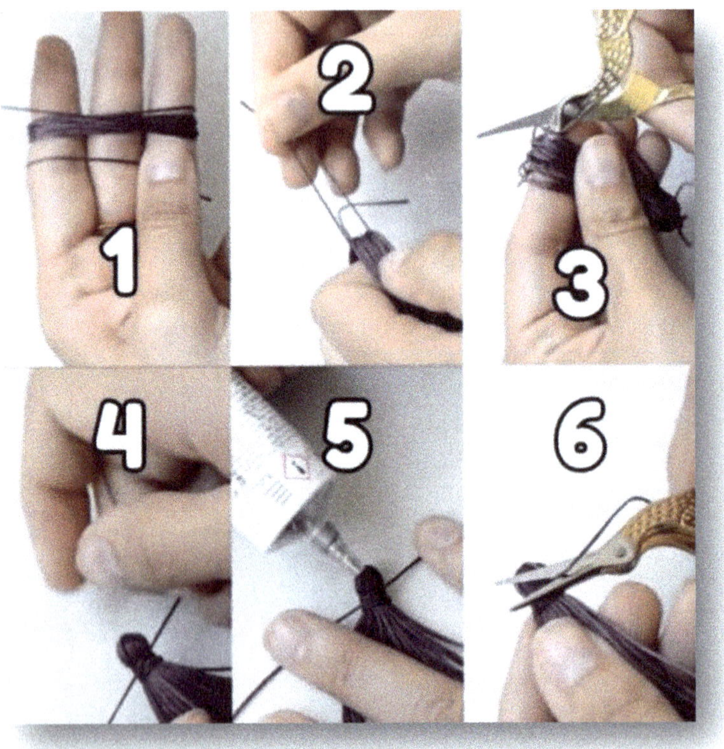

You can reuse old fringes to make earrings. Many garments include fringes as decorative material that you can take advantage of to make your DIY crafts. You can find colored edges on t-shirts, bags, coats, backpacks, or bags of all kinds.

You can recycle colored fringes from clothes you no longer use. Many containers, packs, or T-shirts include these beads.

The exciting thing about making your accessories is to reuse materials and fabrics that you may have forgotten at home. In this way, you contribute to recycling, make responsible consumption, and avoid acquiring unnecessary clothing. If you have fringes, you can also buy them in jewelry bead shops.

Do you prefer to make your fringes? It is effortless, and you need synthetic and resistant thread, contact glue, and scissors.

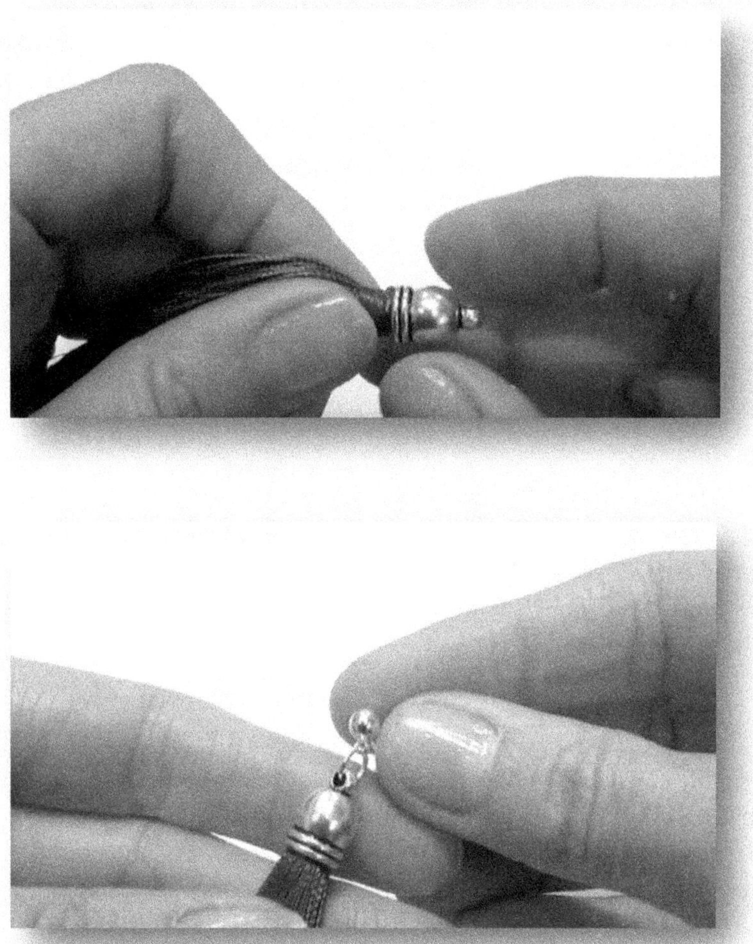

Make your fringe earrings step by step. You only need contact glue, synthetic yarn, and scissors. To complete the ornaments, you will also need jewelry caps and earring hooks.

First of all, wrap 3 meters of thread over your fingers, hold it and tie it with more ribbon, cut the threads on the opposite end, use another piece of string and wrap it around the related part, tie it from behind and use glue to fix the knot. Finally, use scissors to cut the excess piece. At this point, we should already have our two fringes ready to turn them into beautiful earrings. From here, we have several options; the option that we recommend is to use jewelry caps for ornaments and contact glue.

The last step is to use two earring hooks on each cap. You can use jewelry pliers if you need to open and fix the rings or any other material you use.
You can get all the materials used in specialized jewelry stores or by recycling old earrings that you no longer apply.

Choker Necklace

Celtic Choker

Elegant loops allow the emerald and silver beads to stand out, making this a striking piece. The finished length is 12 inches. Be sure to use the ribbon clasp which gives multiple length options to the closure.

Knots Used:

1. Lark's Head Knot
2. Alternating Lark's Head Chain

Supplies:

- 3 strands of black C-Lon cord; two 7ft cords, one 4ft cord
- 18 - green beads (4mm)
- 7 - round silver beads (10 mm)
- Fasteners: Ribbon Clasps, silver
- Glue - Beacon 527 multi-use
- Note: Bead size can vary slightly. Just be sure all beads you choose will slide onto 2 cords.

Instructions:

1. Optional – Find the center of your cord and attach it to the top of the ribbon clasp with a lark's head knot. I found it easier to thread the loose ends through and pull them down until my

loop was near the opening, then push the cords through the loop. Repeat with the 2 remaining strands, putting the four-foot cord in the center. If this is problematic, you could cut all the cords to 7ft and not worry about placement. (If you really trust your glue, you can skip this step by gluing the cords into the clasp and going from there).

2. Lay all cords into the ribbon clasp. Add a generous dap of glue and use pliers to close the clasp.

3. You now have 6 cords to work with. Find the 4 ft. cords and place them in the center. They will be the holding (or filler) cords throughout.

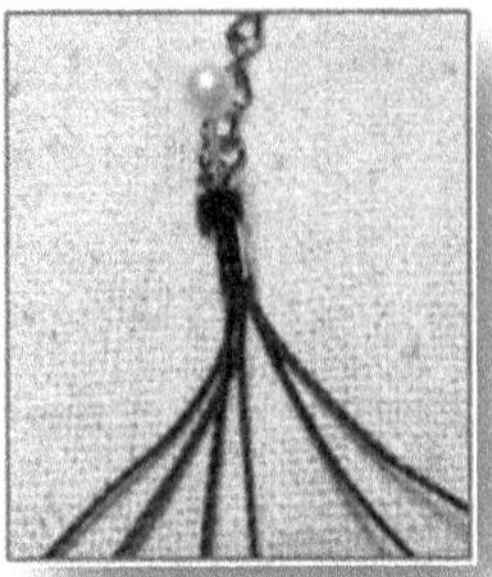

4. Begin your Alternating Lark's Head (ALH) chain, using the outmost right cord then the outermost left cord. Follow with the other right cord then the last left cord. For this first set, the pattern will be hard to see. You may need to tug gently on the cords to get a little slack in them.

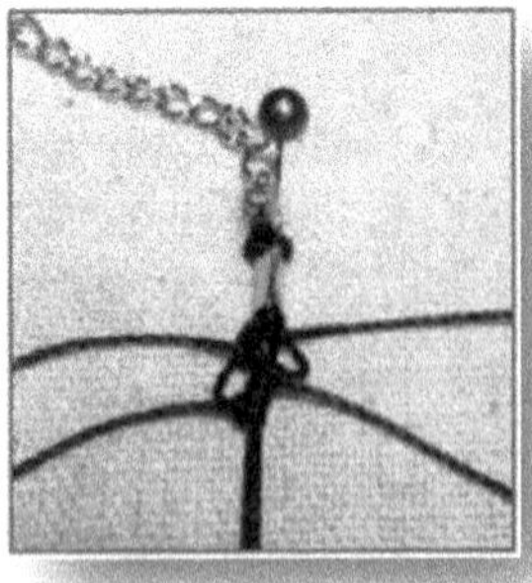

5. Now slide a silver bead onto the center 2 cords.

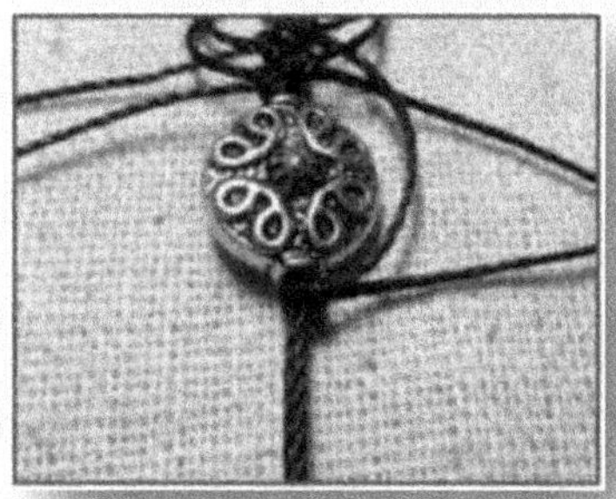

6. The outer cords are now staggered on your holding cords. Continue with the ALH chain by knotting with the upper right cord then tie a knot with the upper left cord.

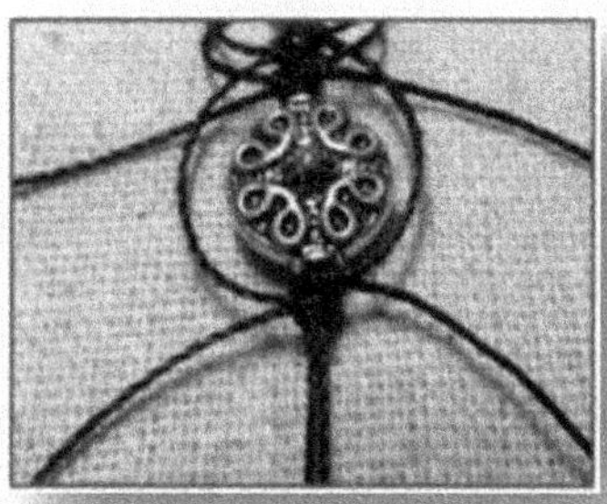

7. Finish your set of 4 knots, then add a green bead

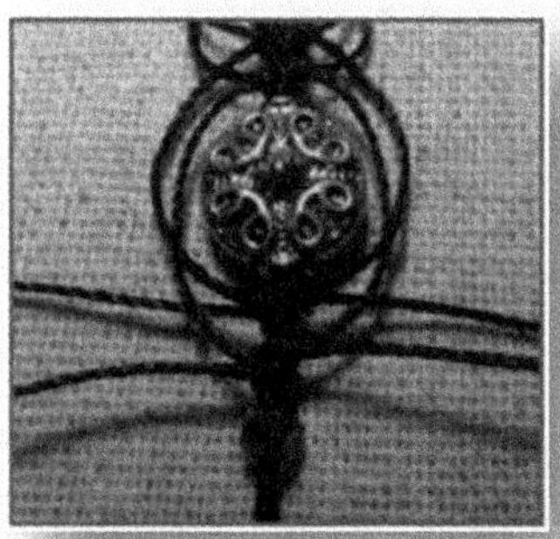

8. Tie four ALH knots followed by a green bead until you have 3 green beads in the pattern. Then tie one more set of 4 ALH knots.

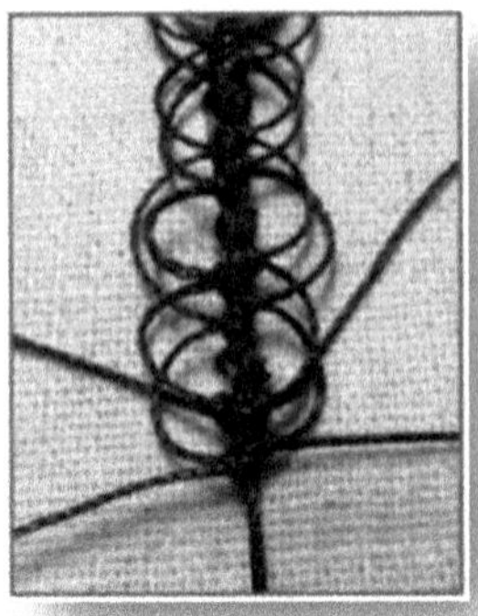

9. Slide on a silver bead and continue creating sequences of 3 green, 1 silver (always with 4 ALH knots between each). End with the 7th silver bead and 1 more set of 4 ALH knots, for a 12" necklace. (Use this to shorten or lengthen as you choose).

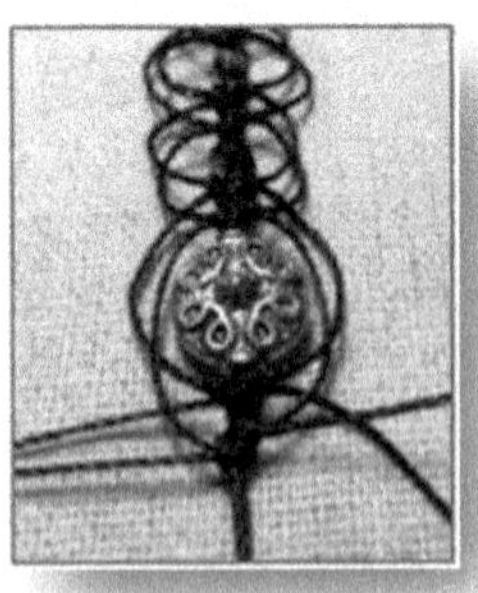

10. Lay all cords in the ribbon clasp and glue well.

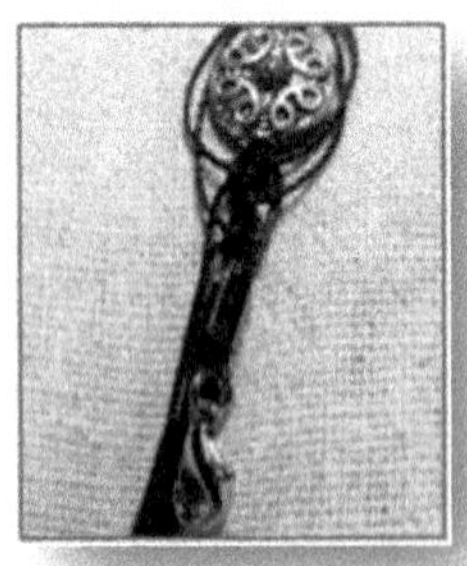

11. Crimp shut and let dry completely. Trim excess cords.

Serenity Bracelet

(Note: if you are familiar with the flat knot, you can move right along into the pattern)

This novice bracelet offers plenty of practice using one of micro macramé's most used knots. You will also gain experience beading and equalizing tension. This bracelet features a button closure and the finished length is 7 inches.

Knots Used:

Flat Knot (aka square knot)

Overhand knot

Supplies:

- White C-Lon cord, 6 ½ ft., x 3
- 18 - Frosted Purple size 6 beads
- 36 - Purple seed beads, size 11
- 1 - 1 cm Purple and white focal bead
- 26 - Dark Purple size 6 beads

- 1 - 5 mm Purple button closure bead

(Note: the button bead needs to be able to fit onto all 6 cords)

Instructions:

1. Take all 3 cords and fold them in half. Find the center and place on your work surface as shown:

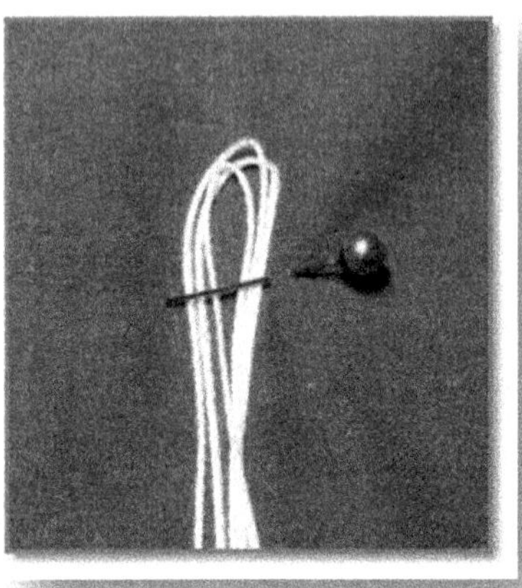

2. Now hold the cords and tie an overhand knot, loosely, at the center point. It should look like this:

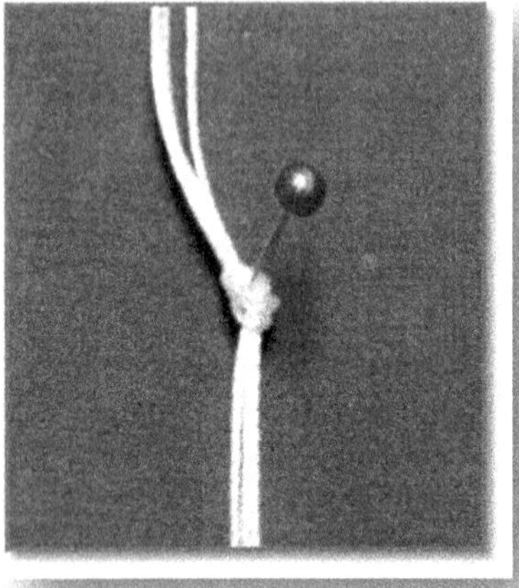

3. We will now make a buttonhole closure. Just below the knot, take each outer cord and tie a flat knot (aka square knot). Continue tying flat knots until you have about 2 ½ cm.

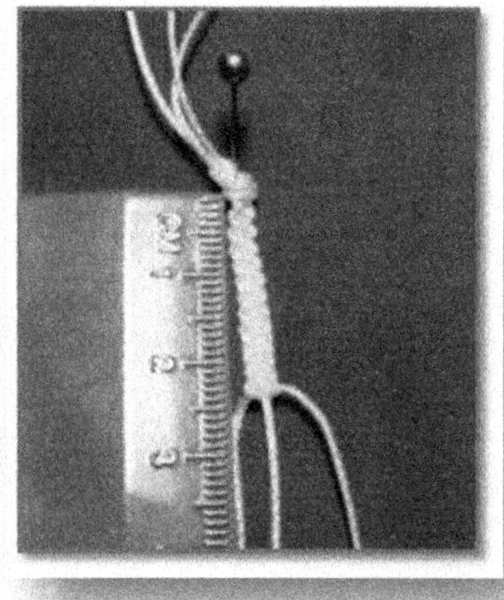

4. Undo your overhand knot and place the ends together in a horseshoe shape.

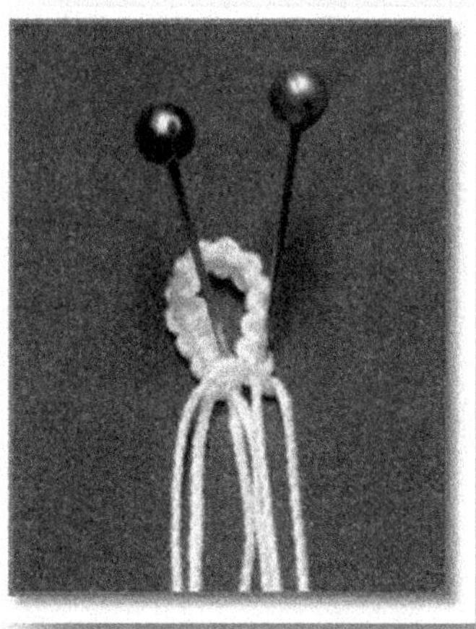

5. We now have all 6 cords together. Think of the cords as numbered 1 through 6 from left to right. Cords 2-5 will stay in the middle as filler cords. Find cord 1 and 6 and use these to tie flat knots around the filler cords. (Note: now you can pass your button bead through the opening to ensure a good fit. Add or subtract flat knots as needed to create a snug fit. This size should be fine for a 5mm bead). Continue to tie flat knots until you have 4 cm worth. (To increase bracelet

length, add more flat knots here, and the equal amount in step 10).

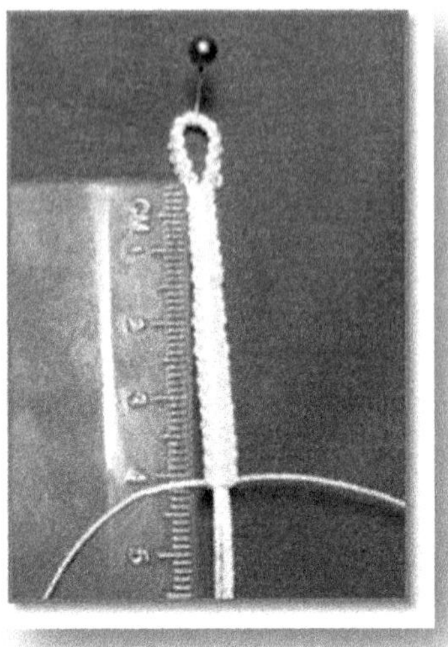

6. 4. Separate cords 1-4-1. Find the center 2 cords. Thread a size 6 frosted purple bead onto them, then tie a flat knot with cords 2 and 5.

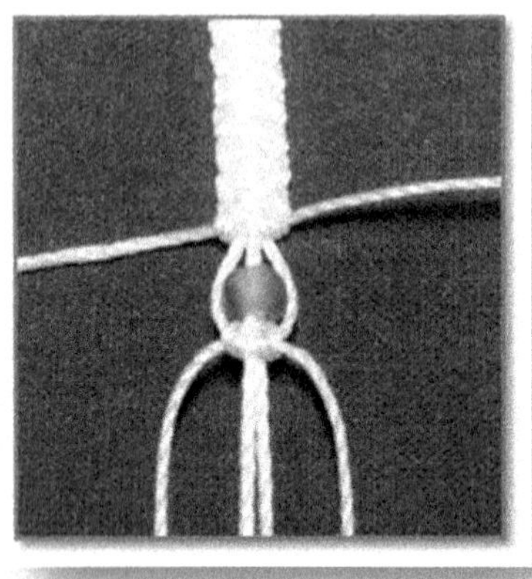

7. 5. We will now work with cords 1 and 6. With cord 1, thread on a seed bead, a dark purple size 6 bead and another seed bead. Repeat with cord 6, then separate the cords into 3-3. Tie

a flat knot with the left 3 cords. Tie a flat knot with the right 3 cords.

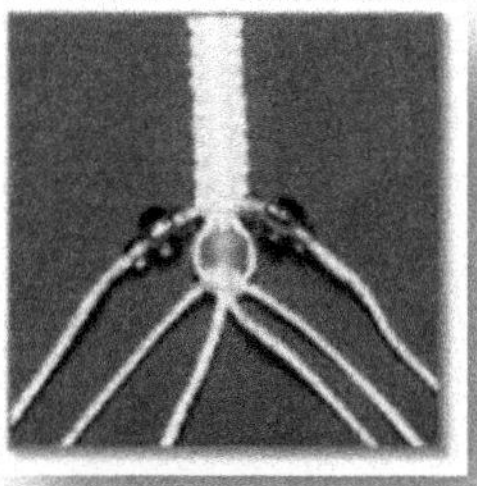

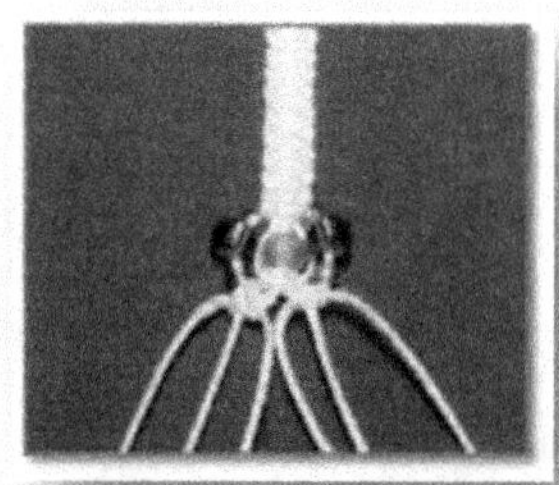

8. 6. Repeat step 4 and 5 three times.

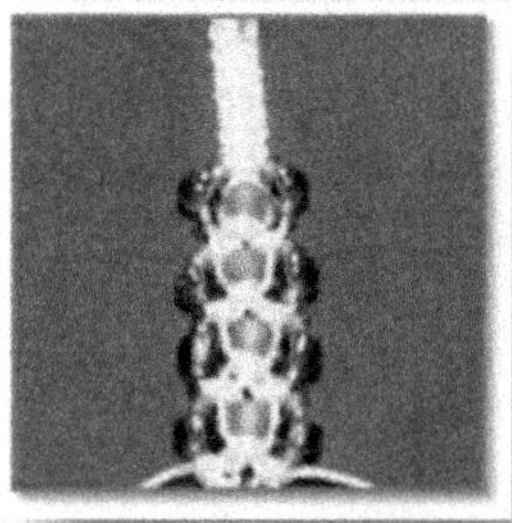

9. Find the center 2 cords, hold together and thread on the 1cm focal bead. Take the cords out (2 and 5) and bead as follows: 2 size 6 dark purple beads, a frosted purple bead, and 2 dark purple beads. Find cords 1 and 6 and bead as follows: 2 frosted purple beads, a seed bead, a dark purple bead, a seed bead, 2 frosted purple beads.

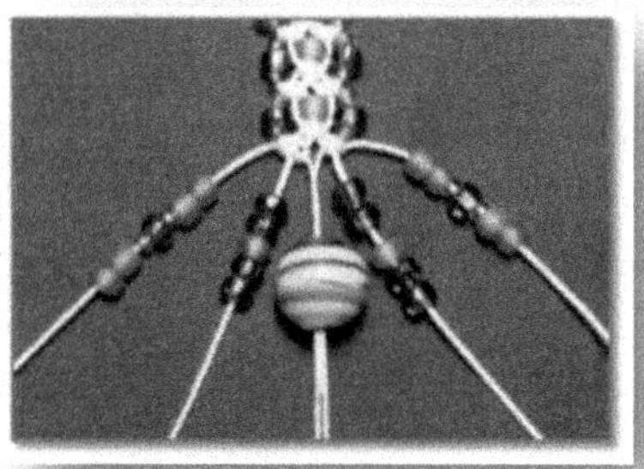

3. With cords 2 and 5, tie a flat knot around the center 2 cords. Place the center 4 cords together and tie a flat knot around them with outer cords 1 and 6.

4. Repeat steps 4 and 5 four times.

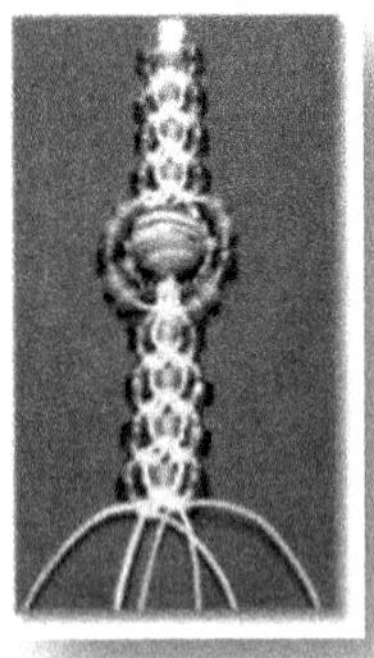

5. Repeat step 3.

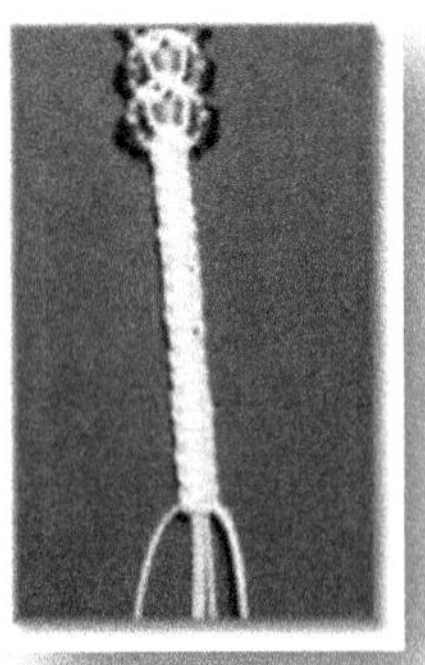

6. Place your button bead on all 6 cords and tie an overhand knot tight against the bead. Glue well and trim the cords.

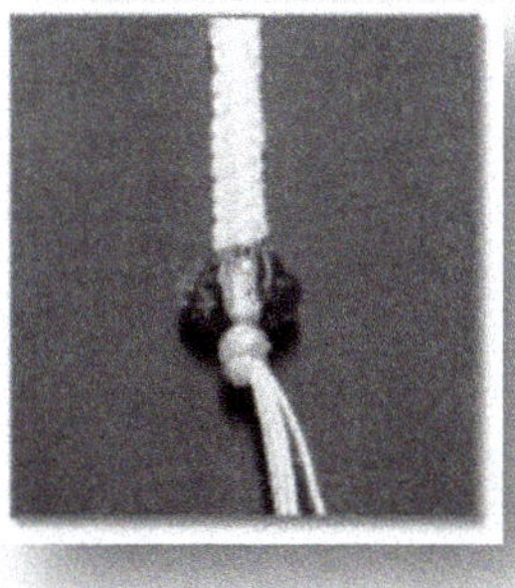

Lantern Bracelet

This pattern may look simply, but please don't try it if you are in a hurry. This one takes patience. Don't worry about getting your picot knots all the exact same shape. Have fun with it! The finished bracelet is 7 ¼ inches in length. If desired, add a picot knot and a spiral knot on each side of the center piece to lengthen it. This pattern has a jump ring closure.

Knots Used: Lark's Head Knot Spiral Knot Picot Knot Overhand Knot

Supplies:

- 3 strands of C-Lon cord (2 light brown and 1 medium brown) 63-inch lengths
- Fasteners (1 jump ring, 1 spring ring or lobster clasp)
- Glue - Beacon 527 multi-use
- 8 small beads (about 4mm) amber to gold colors

- 30 gold seed beads
- 3 beads (about 6 mm) amber color (mine are rectangular, but round or oval will work wonderfully also)
- Note: Bead size can vary slightly. Just be sure all beads you choose will slide onto 2 cords (except seed beads).

Instructions:

1. Find the center of your cord and attach it to the jump ring with a lark's head knot. Repeat with the 2 remaining strands. If you want the 2-tone effect, be sure your second color is NOT placed in the center, or it will only be a filler cord and you will end up with a 1 tone bracelet.

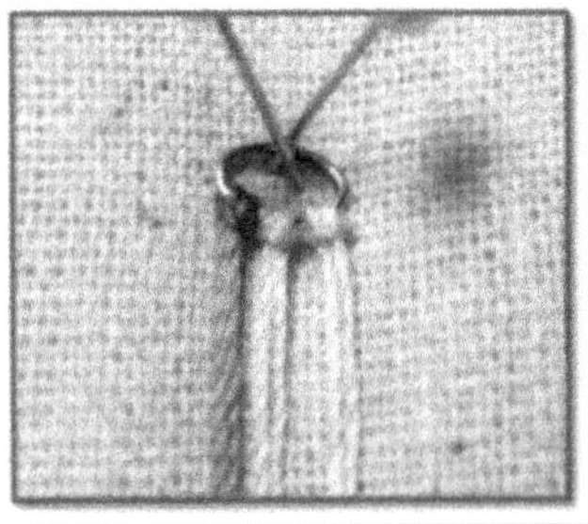

2. You now have 6 cords to work with. Think of them as numbered 1 thorough 6, from left to right. Move cords 1 and 6 apart from the rest. You will use these to work the spiral knot. All others are filler cords. Take cord number 1 tie a spiral knot. Always begin with the left cord. Tie 7 more spirals.

3. Place a 4mm bead on the center 2 cords. Leave cords 1 and 6 alone for now and work 1 flat knot using cords 2 and 5.
4. Now put cords 2 and 5 together with the center strands. Use 1 and 6 to tie a picot flat knot. If you don't like the look of your picot knot, loosen it up and try again. Gently tug the cords into place then lock in tightly with the spiral knot.

Notice here how I am holding the picot knot with my thumbs while pulling the cords tight with my fingers. If you look closely you may be able to see that I have a cord in each hand.

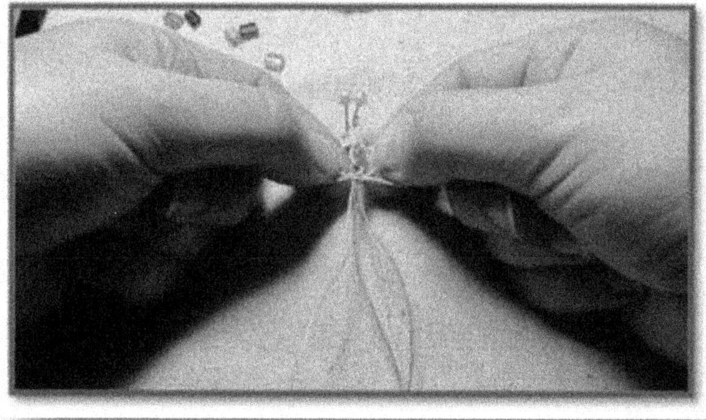

5. Tie 8 spiral knots (using left cord throughout pattern).
6. Place a 4mm bead on the center 2 cords. Leave cords 1 and 6 alone for now and work 1 flat knot using cords 2 and 5. Now put cords 2 and 5 together with the center strands. Use strands 1 and 6 to tie a picot flat knot.
7. Repeat steps 5 and 6 until you have 5 sets of spirals.

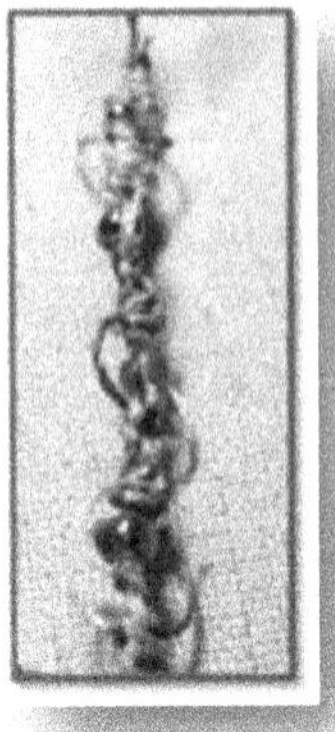

8. Place 5 seed beads on cords 1 and 6. Put cords 3 and 4 together and string on a 6 mm bead. Tie one flat knot with the outermost cords.

Repeat this step two more times.

Now repeat steps 5 and 6 until you have 5 sets of spirals from the center point. Thread on your clasp. Tie an overhand knot with each cord and glue well. Let dry completely. As this is the weakest point in the design, I advise trimming the excess cords and gluing again. Let dry.

Macramé Earrings are great because they're definitely not like your usual boring, silver or gold earrings. From neon ones to the more subdued and elegant, you'll surely find the right Macramé Earrings for you! Try these ones, and see for yourself!

Day Glow Earrings

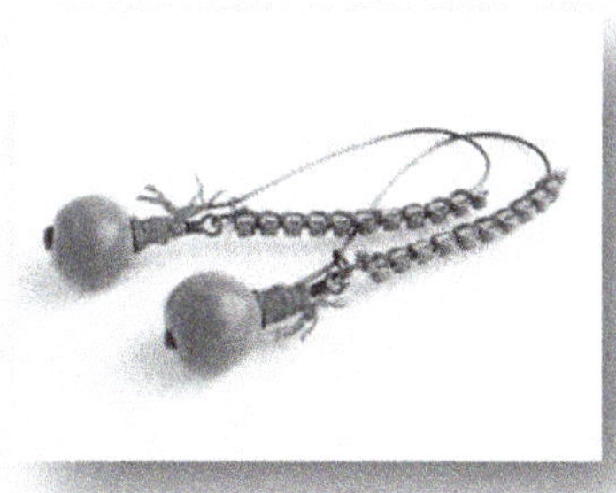

What you need:

- 36" Irish-waxed linen cord
- 3" 2.5mm crystal chain
- 2 3" headpins
- 2 large kidney ear wires
- 2 12mm beads
- Scissors
- Cutters
- Round nose pliers

- Chain nose pliers

Instructions:

1. Tie an overhand knot by using 18" waxed linen, and make sure to leave 3". Make sure it reaches 1 headpin.

2. String ceramic on both ends of the cord, then wrap the headpin with a long cord.
3. Then, tie the ends of the cords together using a square knot, and make sure to wrap the loop.

4. On top of 1 kidney wire, hold a 1 ½" of crystal chain. Place the rest of the waxed linen under the crystal and let it go criss-cross around the ear wire.
5. End the loop with a square knot and clean the ends by trimming them.
6. Put the beaded dangle onto the wire.

As for the second earring, you should String ceramic on both ends of the cord, then wrap the headpin with a long cord. Then, tie the ends of the cords together using a square knot, and make sure to wrap the loop. On top of 1 kidney wire, hold a 1 ½" of crystal chain. Place the rest of the waxed linen under the crystal and let it go criss-cross around the ear wire.
End the loop with a square knot and clean the ends by trimming them, as well.

Macramé Spiral Earrings

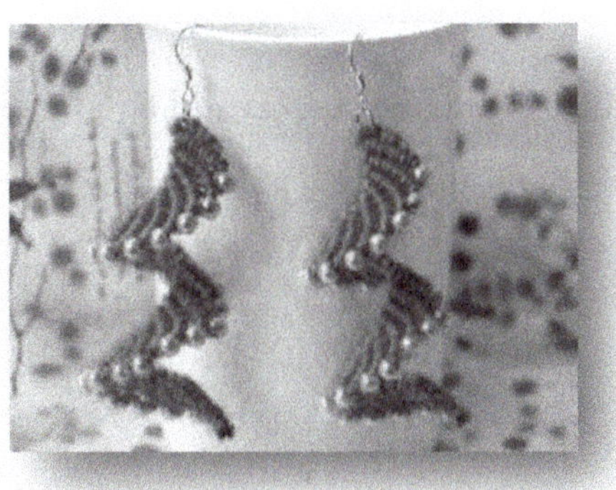

Now, you wouldn't have to imagine seashells by the seashore as you can already wear them—or at least, a Macramé version of them! If this does not remind you of shells, maybe it will remind you of fun parties or spiral stairs. Either way, it's a fun necklace to look at—and to wear, as well!

What you need:

- Lighter
- Earring hooks
- Jump rings
- 4mm light cyan glass pearl
- 1 mm nylon thread

Instructions:

1. Cut three pieces of nylon thread at 100 cm. One of these would be the nylon thread and the rest would both be the working threads. A crown knot should then be tied around the holding thread.

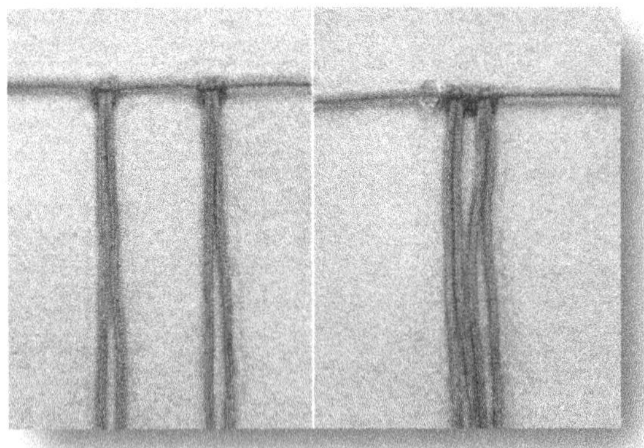

2. Check the left holding thread and make sure to add a jump ring there.

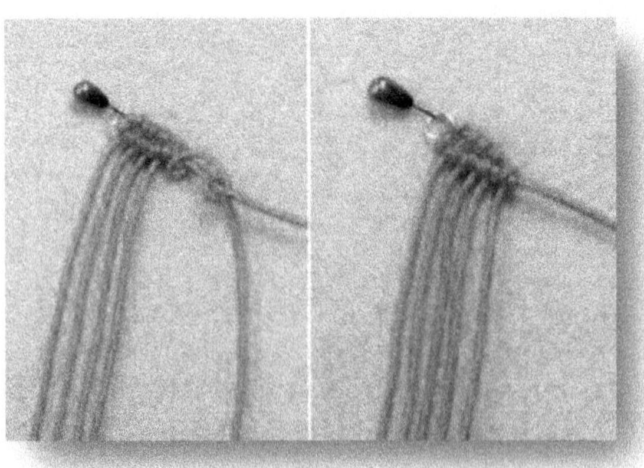

3. Over the four working threads, go ahead and place the left holding thread there. Use the four working threads to hold the thread and the make a half hitch knot on the remaining thread.
4. Tie 4 half hitch knots on the leftmost thread and then slide a pearl onto the nylon thread. Secure with a half hitch knot.

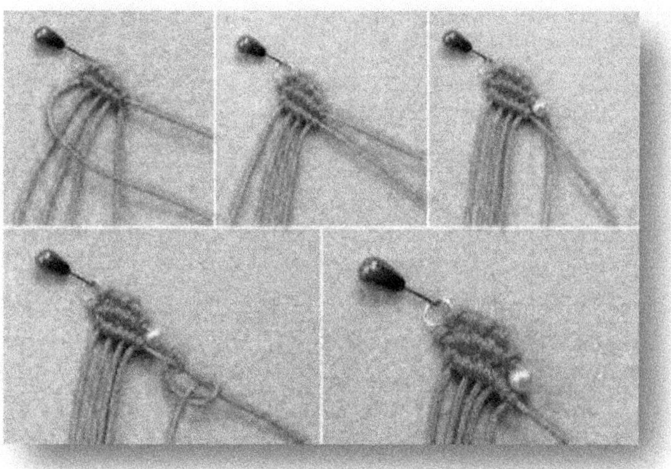

5. Repeat for 25 times to create a perfect spiral.

6. To fasten, get your holding thread again (the leftmost thread, in this case), and let it overlap the thread you are currently holding. Cut one holding thread after tying a half hitch knot.

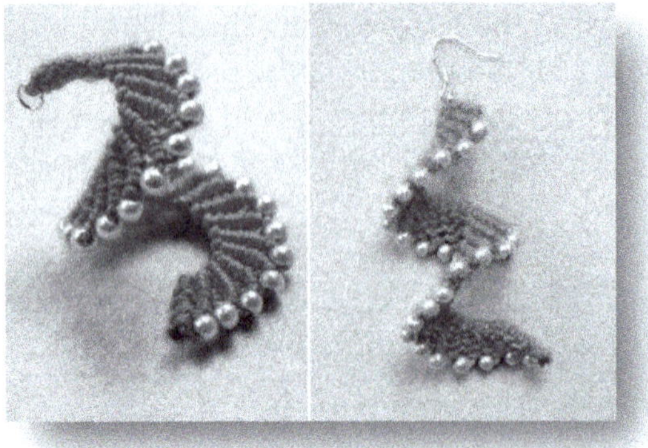

7. Tie two more half hitch knots and slide a pearl onto the rightmost thread. Make sure to use the thread in a half hitch again.
8. To finish, just cut some extra threads off and burn the ends with a lighter. Make sure to attach earring hooks, as well.

Summery Chevron Earrings

This one is something that you could make a lot of as it could serve as friendship earrings for you and the ones you love. It's very summery, and really colorful—which makes it total eye candy! You'd surely love making and wearing this one!

What you need:

- Ear wires
- Small chain

- Nylon/yarn (or any cord you want)
- Wire
- Pliers
- Scissors
- Hot glue gun

Instructions:

1. Fold the cord into four, and then tie a base/square knot as you hold the four lengths. Once you do this, you'll notice that you have eight pieces of cotton lengths with you. What you should do is separate them into twos, and tie a knot in each of those pairs before you start knotting with the square knot. It's like you're making a friendship bracelet!

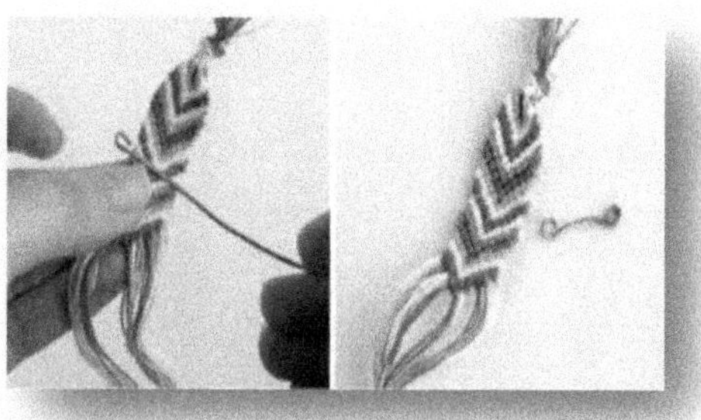

2. Use the wire to make two loops out of the thread and make sure the center and sides have the same width.

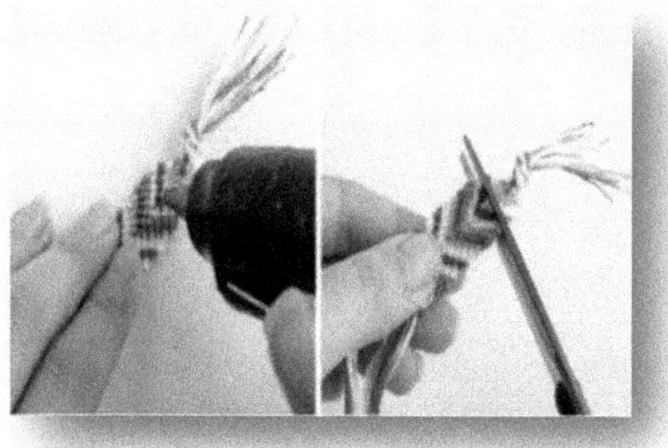

3. At the back of the bracelet, make use of hot glue to prevent knots from spooling.

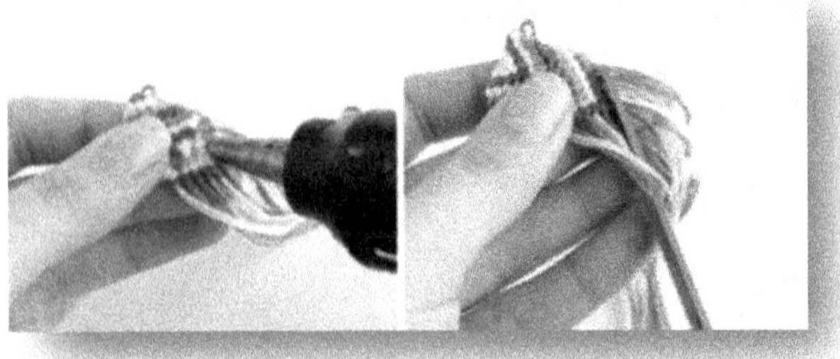

4. Fold the bracelet around the wire shortly after putting some glue and letting it cool.

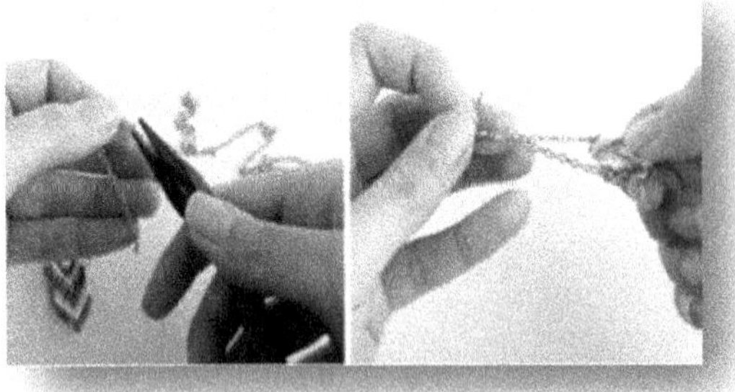

5. Use hot glue so knots wouldn't come down again. Make sure to cut the excess thread.
6. Cut the chain to your desired length—or how you want the earrings to look like. Secure the ear wire as you find the middle of the chain.

7. Enjoy your new earrings!

Hearty Paperclip Earrings

Now this one is really creative because it makes use of various embroidery threads and paper clips to give you earrings unlike any other. If you think paper clips are just basic school supplies, well, think again.

What you need:

- Paper clips
- Embroidery thread
- Earring hooks
- Glue
- Water
- Paint brush

Instructions:

1. Bend some paper clips until they resemble hearts. Take note that you may have to try a lot of times because it's expected that you may not get the effect right away. Once you have made some hearts, glue the ends to keep them secure.

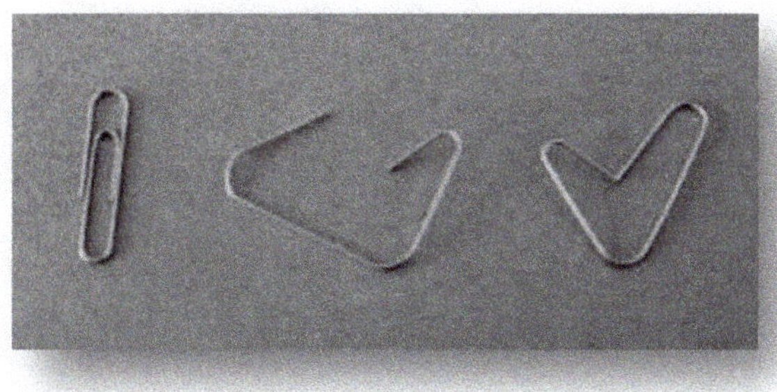

2. Wrap embroidery thread just to coat the clips, and then leave some inches of thread hanging so you could make half-hitch knots out of them.

3. Tie knots until you reach the end and paint with a mix of water and glue to keep secure.

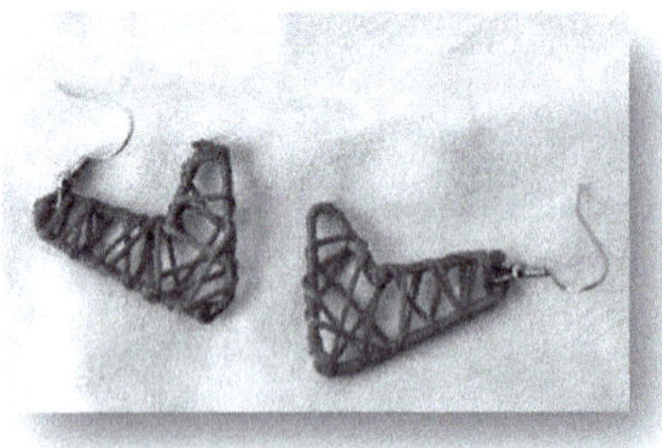

4. Let dry and then add the earring hooks.

Fringe Fun Earrings

These earrings could surely add a lot of fun to your ears! They're perfect reminders of festivals, or fun afternoons drinking cocktails and punch with your favorite people!

What you need:

- 56" of 4-ply Irish waxed linen cord
- 2 brass headpins
- 2 brass ear wires
- 2 hammered brass 33mm metal rings
- 22 glass 6mm rounds
- Round nose pliers
- Chain nose pliers
- scissors

Instructions:

1. Make eye pins out of the headpins by bending the tip and making a loophole, just like what's shown below.

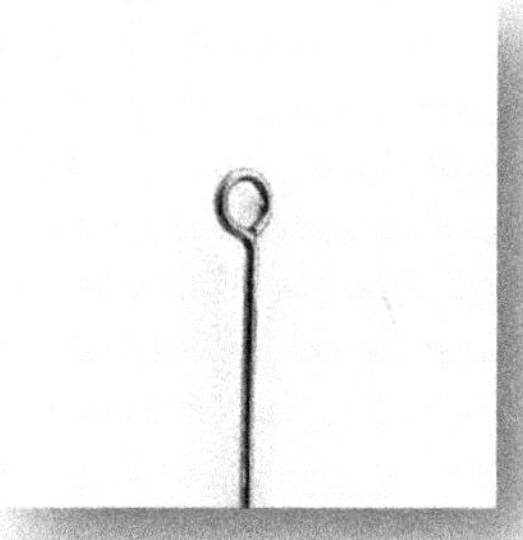

2. String a glass round to form a single loop and then set aside before cutting in half.

3. At the end of one cord, make a 3" fold and then go and knot around the brass ring.

4. Use the long end of the cord to make two half-hitch knots just around the ring.

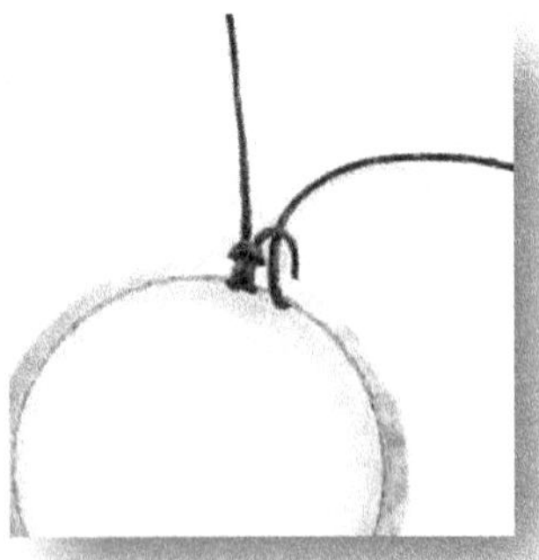

5. String a glass bead so that you could form an overhead knot. Trim until you reach 1/8" and the make an overhand knot again. Trim once more to 1/8".

6. Repeat these steps (with the exception of the first one) and then attach the bead link to the brass ring.

7. Repeat all the steps to make the second earring.

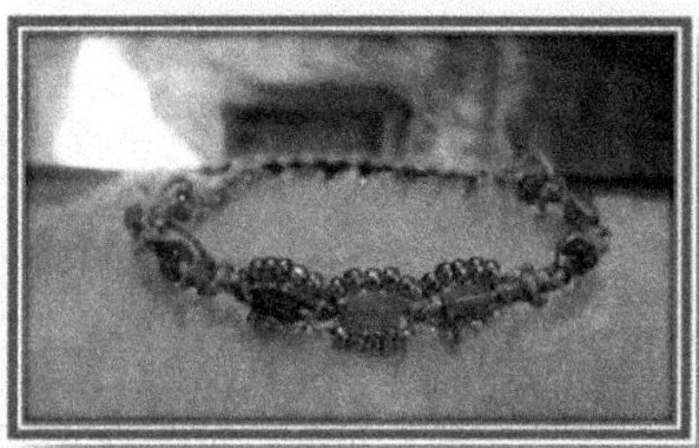

This pattern may look simple, but please don't try it if you are in a hurry. This one takes patience. Don't worry about getting your picot knots all the exact same shape. Have fun with it! The finished bracelet is 7 ¼ inches in length. If desired, add a picot knot and a spiral knot on each side of the center piece to lengthen it. This pattern has a jump ring closure.

Knots Used: Lark's Head Knot Spiral Knot Picot Knot Overhand Knot

Supplies:

- 3 strands of C-Lon cord (2 light brown and 1 medium brown) 63 inch lengths
- Fasteners (1 jump ring, 1 spring ring or lobster clasp)
- Glue - Beacon 527 multi-use
- 8 small beads (about 4mm) amber to gold colors
- 30 gold seed beads

- 3 beads (about 6 mm) amber color (mine are rectangular, but round or oval will work wonderfully also)

Note: Bead size can vary slightly. Just be sure all beads you choose will slide onto 2 cords (except seed beads).

Instructions:

1. Find the center of your cord and attach it to the jump ring with a lark's head knot. Repeat with the 2 remaining strands. If you want the 2 tone effect, be sure your second color is Not placed in the center, or it will only be a filler cord and you will end up with a 1 tone bracelet.

2. You now have 6 cords to work with. Think of them as numbered 1 thorough 6, from left to right. Move cords 1 and 6 apart from the rest. You will use these to work the spiral knot. All others are filler cords. Take cord number 1 tie a spiral knot. Always begin with the left cord. Tie 7 more spirals.

3. Place a 4mm bead on the center 2 cords. Leave cords 1 and 6 alone for now and work 1 flat knot using cords 2 and 5.
4. Now put cords 2 and 5 together with the center strands. Use 1 and 6 to tie a picot flat knot. If you don't like the look of your

picot knot, loosen it up and try again. Gently tug the cords into place then lock in tightly with the next spiral knot.

Notice here how I am holding the picot knot with my thumbs while pulling the cords tight with my fingers. If you look closely you may be able to see that I have a cord in each hand.

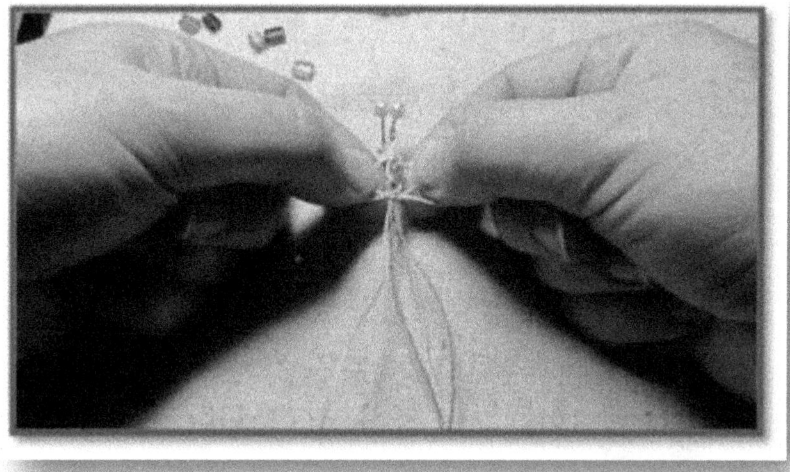

5. Tie 8 spiral knots (using left cord throughout pattern).
6. Place a 4mm bead on the center 2 cords. Leave cords 1 and 6 alone for now and work 1 flat knot using cords 2 and 5. Now put cords 2 and 5 together with the center strands. Use strands 1 and 6 to tie a picot flat knot.
7. Repeat steps 5 and 6 until you have 5 sets of spirals.

8. Next place 5 seed beads on cords 1 and 6. Put cords 3 and 4 together and string on a 6 mm bead. Tie one flat knot with the outermost cords.

9. Repeat this step two more times.

10. Now repeat steps 5 and 6 until you have 5 sets of spirals from the center point, thread on your clasp. Tie an overhand knot with each cord and glue well. Let dry completely. As this is the weakest point in the design, I advise trimming the excess cords and gluing again. Let dry.

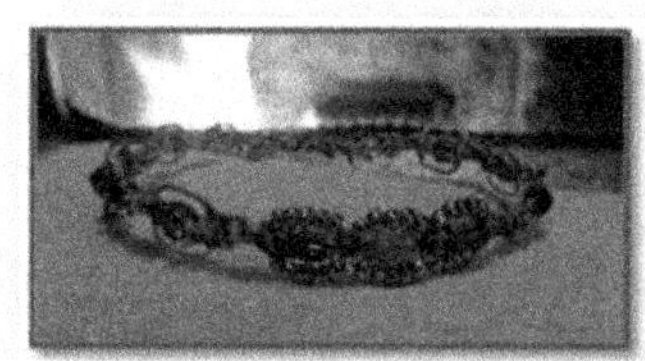

Chapter 5: Make a Hanger for Your Wooden Dowel

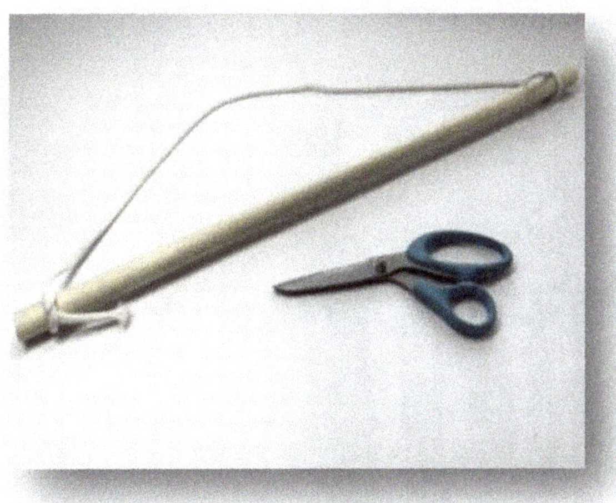

Cut a piece of macramé cord that is three feet (1 meter) and tied to a wooden dowel. Connect the two sides of the wooden dowel to each end of the thread.You are going to use this to mount your macramé project when it is over. In the beginning, I like to attach it, so I can hang up the macramé project when I tie knots. It is much easier to work this way than to determine it.

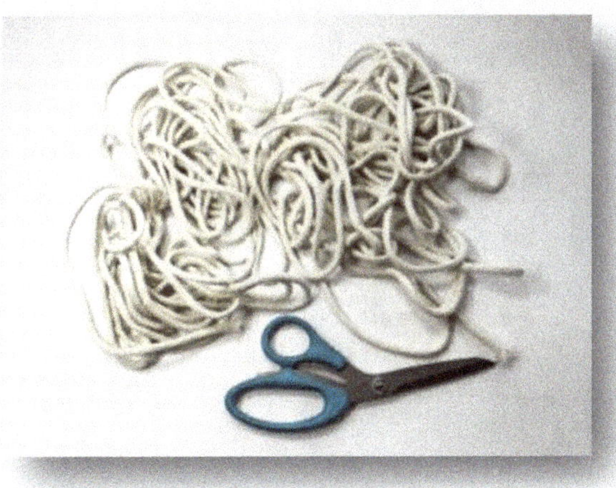

Cut your macramé rope into 12 string lengths 15 feet (4.5 meters) long with the pair of scissors. It might sound like a lot of rope, but knots

take up more cord than you expect. If you need it, there's no way to make the rope thicker, so you better cut it than you will.
Fold one of the macramé cores in half on the wooden dowel and use a ladle's head knot to tie it to a wooden dowel.
Join the other cords in the same way

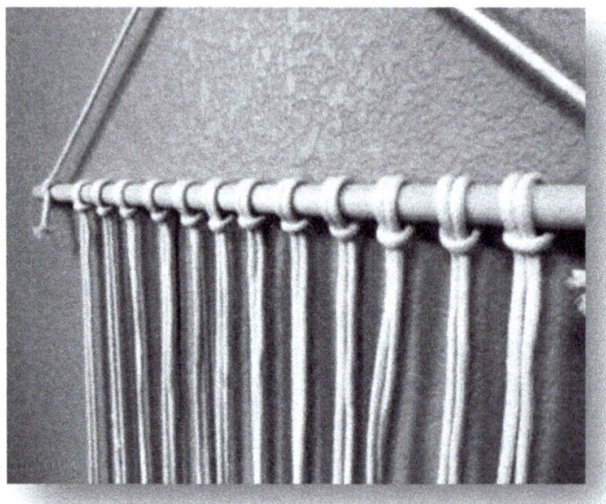

Take the first four strings and make left facing spiral stitch (also referred to as a half-knot Lynton) by tying 13 half knots.

Using four rope to make a further spiral stitch of 13 half knots using the same pair of four ropes. Continue to work in four-chord. You should have a minimum of six spiral stitches before you finish.

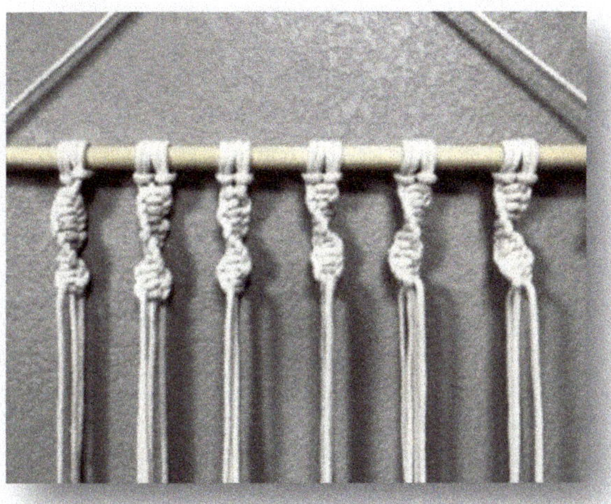

Scale about two inches down from the last knot in a spiral point. This is where your knot, the square knot, will be found.
Make a right knot profile with the first four strings. Continue to make the correct knots face throughout this row. Do your best to keep them all even horizontally. You're going to end up with six knots together.
The second row of square knots now is the time to start the square knots so we can have the knots "V" shape

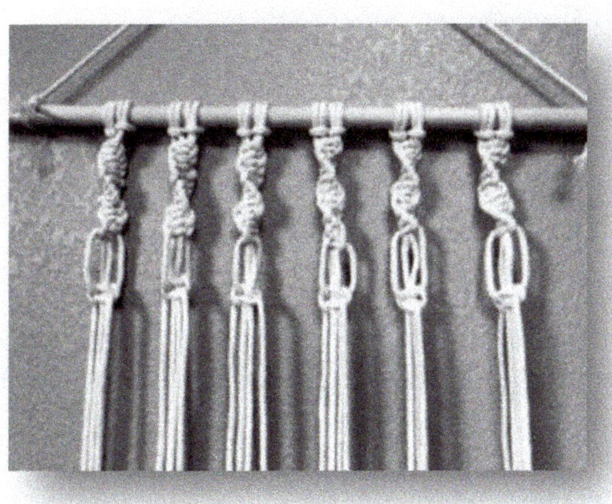

Set open the first two strings and the last two strings. Consider each group of four right-facing square knots. You now have a second line with the first two and last two unknotted cords and five square knots. It doesn't matter how you space them; just keep them for each row together.

Keep Decreasing the Square knots A "V" formed from the square knots in the third row, the first four strings and the last four strings will be left out. You're going to have four knots together. For the fourth row at the top, leave six cords and at the end six cords. You're going to have 3 square ties. In the fifth row, in the beginning, you'll have eight cords and at the end eight cords. Now you're going to have two square ties. For the sixth and final row, ten cords at the beginning and ten cords at the end are to be released. It lets you make a last square knot with four strings.

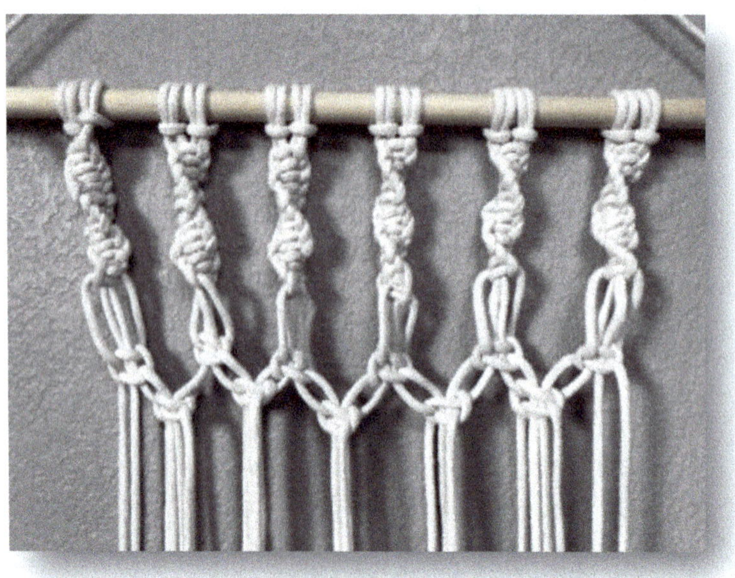

Square Knots Square Making a second "V' in square knots time we'll increase them into a triangle or an upside-down" V "For this first segment, bring out the first eight and last eight cords. That will make two square knots.

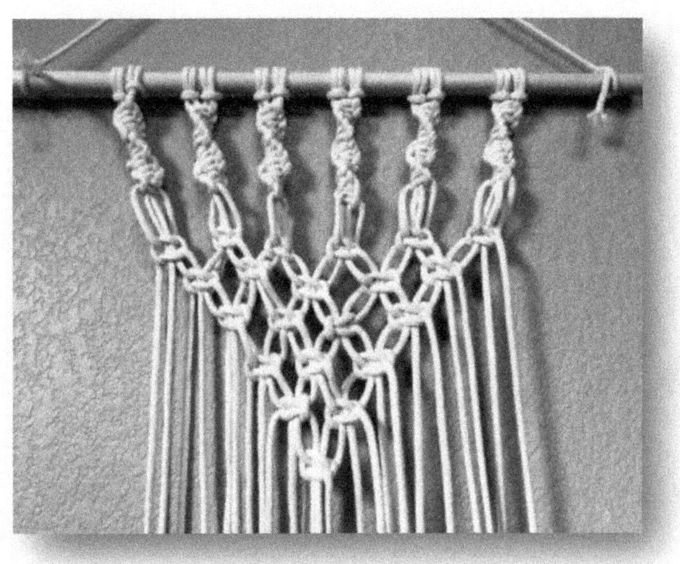

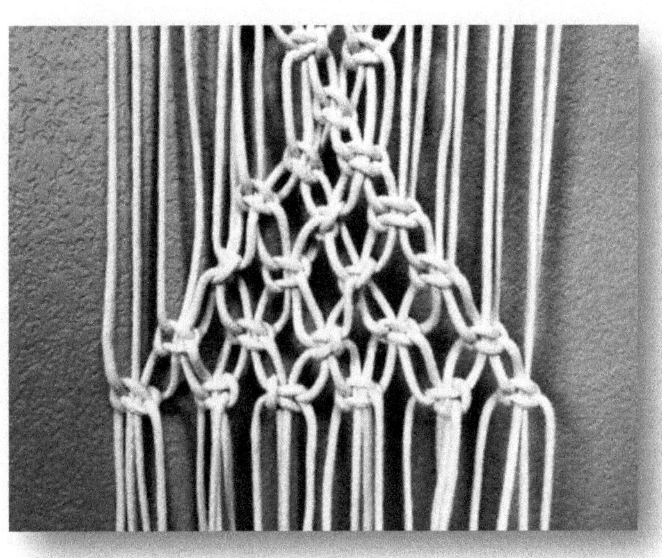

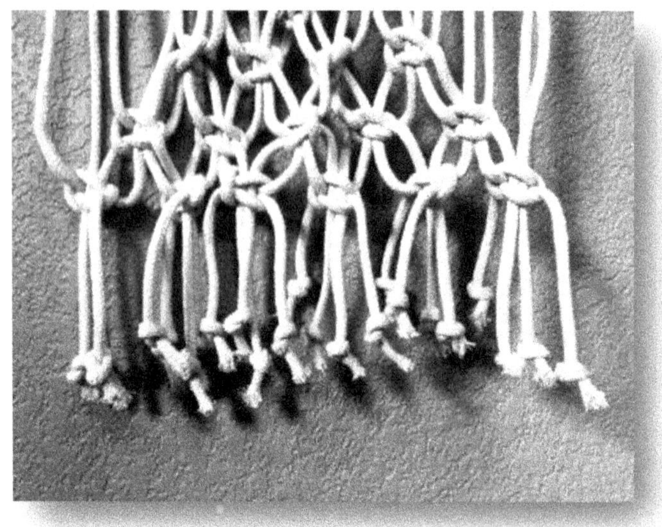

You already know the term macramé whether you grew up in the 1970s or have been on Pinterest for several years. Macramé models have elaborate designs with a variety of knots which come in different shapes and sizes.

The most common examples on the internet are wall hangings, but with this technique and material, you can do much more. And while we're still looking forward to one of these exciting projects, we have decided to move the focus away from the wall and to more practical concepts.

Such macramé tutorials are ideal for beginners, and some of them can be completed without a single node. A demonstration lacks nodes at all but uses macramé cord for spinning instead. Would you like to learn more? See below favorite examples.

Nonetheless, first, learn how to make a few simple macramé knots before you launch any of the following projects. Practice these knots until you are confident in the result as much as possible.

A macramé Table Runner

A Beautiful Mess Most macramé table runners are out there, but we love that by A Beautiful Mess. The photos break the pattern into simple steps, and the instructions are straightforward. It can be challenging to figure out how to make a knot without a recording, but these pictures give you a good idea of what every knot will look like.

I talk in layers of co-ordination and contrasts when decorating every room. Such three elements that make a room less simple, regardless of whether it is color, texture or scale. My fourth guideline is polyvalence! This macramé table runner checked all boxes and made this compact nook with its basic and intriguing style even more unique.

All you need to know is three essential nodes, and you have a charming layer that works every season. If you know the knots learned here, you can tailor your table runner to the length of your table or change it totally and create a hanging macramé wall.

Supply: -12" wooden dowel –22 lengths of cotton rope measuring 3 mm –with cotton twine over the door–2" with dowel hanger scissors

Step One: Apply cotton twine to each end of the dowel and hang it on the door hanger. Fold your first 16" rope strand in half and create a knot on your dowel. For even more thorough measures, see this article.

Step Two: Keep each 16' rope strand with a lark's head knot until you have a total of 22. This will allow you to work with 44 strands.

Step 3: Cast the outside right cable across all the other cables (left) and drop the end of your door handle. This will form the basis of the series of knots known as a half-hitch to build a horizontal row. From the right side, use the second rope to tie a knot around the rope you have just draped so that it's 6" below the dowel.

Step Four: Use the same beach to tie a second knot to the foundation line. This is regarded as a halving knot.

Step Five: Make sure they are clear and even.

Step Six: Repeat from the outside with the second, third and fourth ropes and tie another hitch-knot, so it is snug, etc. You're going to begin to see the trend. It's a half-hitch horizontal.

Step 7: Continue to tie successive cords throughout a single knot. You don't want to be so close that it's at the edges in the distance.

Step 8: From the right again, use the four outer strands to build a knot about 1.5" below the horizontal knots. See this macramé storage article for more information on a square knot.

Out the four (five to eight) strands then tie another knot of nine to twelve strands. Keep skipping four before you cross the line.

Step Nine: begin again on the right, use the four strands that you skipped (five to eight) and tie a square knot about 3" below the dowel.

Step Ten: Continue tying four-strand sets in square knots until the row is ended.

Chapter 6: Hammock Chair

Materials Required:

- Cord Length (size: 6 mm)
- Two 3-inch (heavy-duty) welded metal loop
- Elastic tape measure
- Cloth glue that dries completely

Knots used:

- Wrapped Knot
- Overhand Knot
- Barrel Knot
- Larks Head Knot
- Double Half Hitch (DHH)
- Alternating Square Knots (ASK)

Preparation (Cut the cords as follows):

- 16 strings, each of size 3.5 yards for upper side support
- 16 cords, each of size 4.5 yards for lower side support
- 32 strings, each of size 7 yards the seat
- Two strings, each of size 50 inches these would be for wrapping knots.

Step by Step Instructions:

1. Move 8 of the 4.5-yard cords into the ring then connect the ends. Tie the knots around the fence. Place on top of the previously bound cords 8 of the 3.5-yard cords, then fold and arrange them as well. Tie a knot wrapped around the strings, as laid out below:

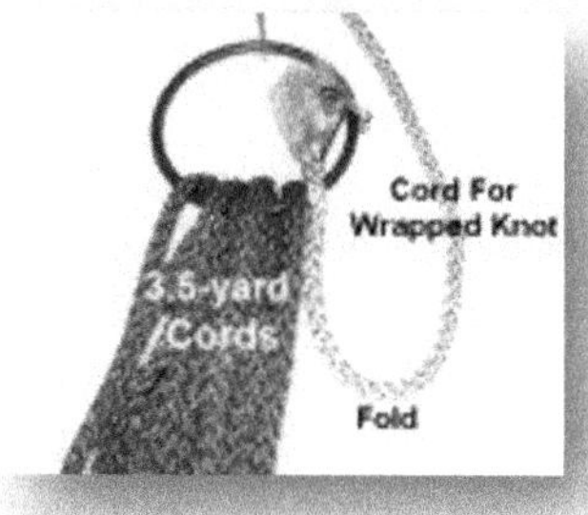

2. Tie one side of a 50-inch chord to the right of the folded cords beside the bell. Move 2 inches down and continue winding this cord around the remainder of the cords. Restore the work-end to the area near the triangle.
3. Tie the working end around the strings, and also the locked end of the working string. Wrap firmly, then begin to push forward when near to the ground.

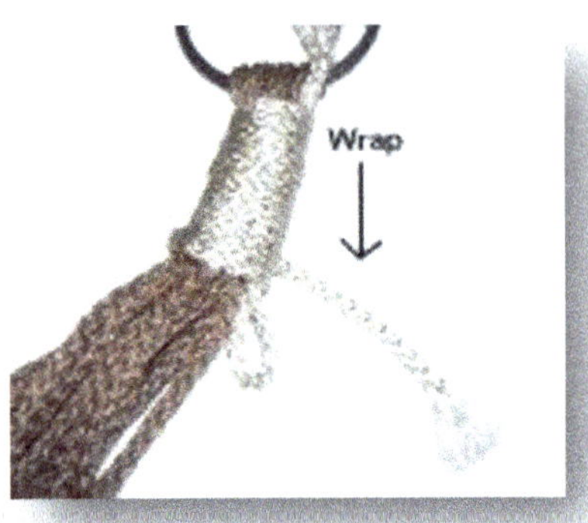

4. The folded part of Working Cord now looks like a shell. Across this loop move the working end of the working thread.

5. Pull the sealed portion, at the top binding point. This will push the end of the job by the Wrapped Knot, and the revolving circle formed by the working rope. Trim all of the cord flush's loose ends with both the top and bottom edges and drape the stubs inside where they are not noticeable. The resulting knot looks like the one on the pic.

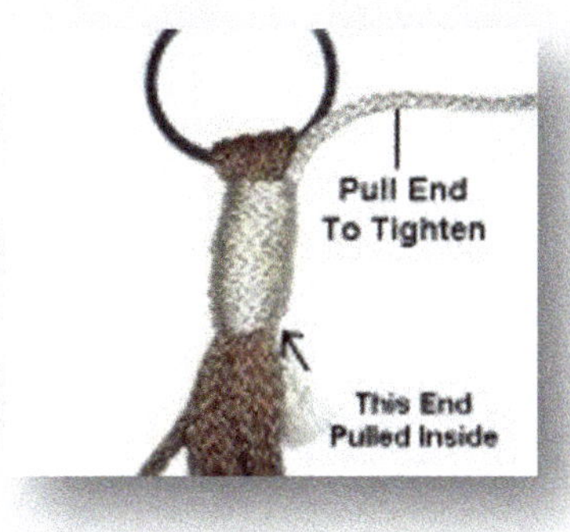

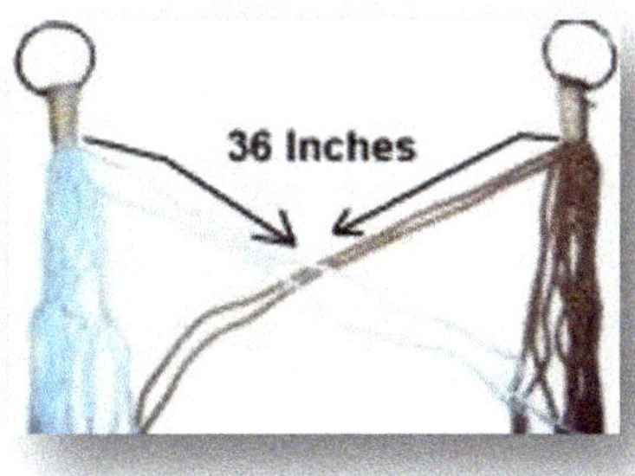

6. Recreate step 1, connecting the remaining 3.5-yard and 4.5-yard cords onto the other loop in the same manner. CAREFULLY take both rings on each string, and they keep the ring securely. They shouldn't trip on rings back and forth. Connect the links to the desk floor, or put them up such that the cords are in an upright position. Choose 2 of the shorter strings from the right side ring (3.5 yard), and two more from the left side ring. The strings you choose will settle wherever they come off the Wrapped Knot. These cords are to act as supporting loops to the upper side of the Hammock Frame. Move down 36 inches from the bottom edge of the Wrapped Knot. The four cords are to be kept diagonally to each other, and they unite at this point. That would form the upper edge of your chair's back.Mentally mark the left side cables as 1 and 2, and the right as 3 and 4. Crawl a simple Square knot using them. The active cables are 1 and 4, and the fillers are 2 and 3. To build the back and bottom of the Hammock Chair, you must connect the other strings on each side of this Knot.

Hold the numbered ENDS to recall which cables to use in your next move. The result would be similar to the one in the photo below.

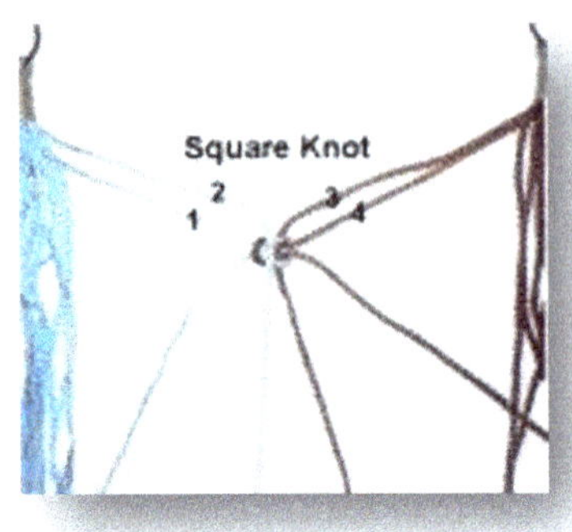

7. Move the ends of the four strings to the right and south, standing parallel to the section that descends from the rings. For all these four lines the back and seat cords of the Hammock Chair should be connected. Authors tip: This is best to operate on a flat floor, because it allows to conveniently place the lines, because the wires are horizontal. Curl one 7-yard string in half and put it on top of the four holding strings on the Square knot's left. The fold is to be aimed at you. Take the halves under the holding cords and over the folded field and pull them to you. This knot is the Larks Head Knot (LHK) in reverse. Leave a tiny gap on the holding cord between the knot and the Square knot. Knots should be tightened.

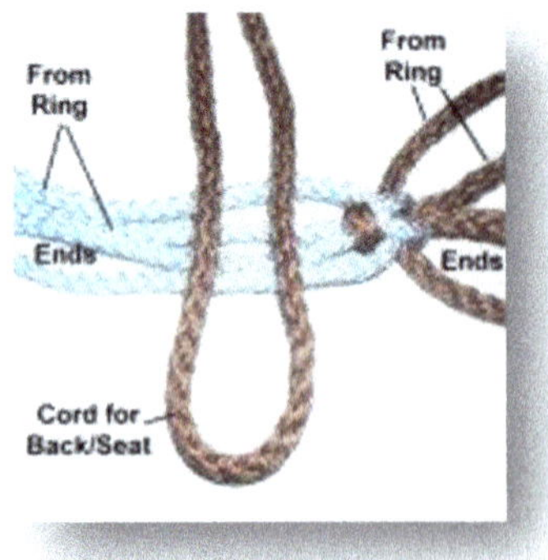

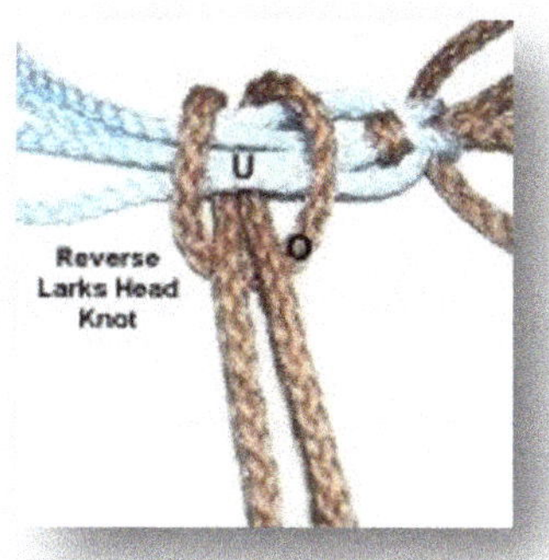

8. Tie the right half of the rope with a Half Hitch tie, by placing it to the right of the Larks Head tie. Pass it through the carrying strings, and then beneath. Place it around the operating cord when you bring it in next to you. Knot must be tighten.Now use the left half of the working cord to make a Half Hop on the Larks Head knot to the top. Tighten the knot in the same fashion as previously achieved. Move to the right of top. Tighten the knot in the same fashion as previously achieved. Move to the right of yard cords left over.A minimum of 16 cables will be placed in the middle of the holding cords on either side of the SK. It is important that you calculate carefully at this stage, so that the ASK rows are matched correctly. Accurately calculate the number of sections, and the gaps are equivalent to the amount of side aids that you intend to deal with.

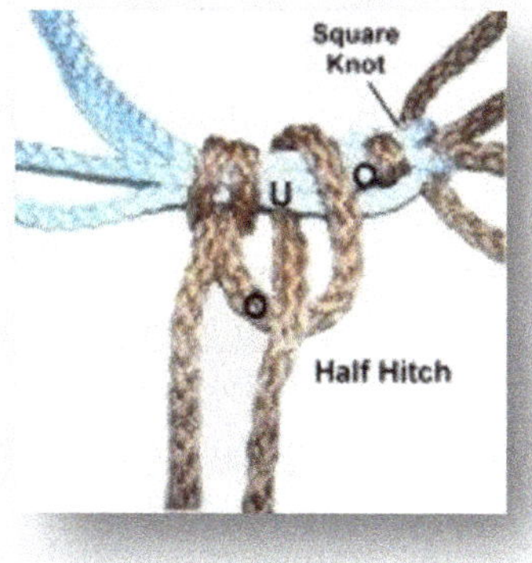

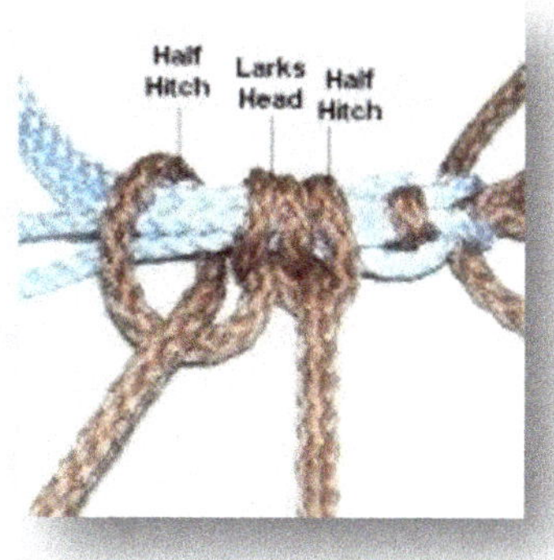

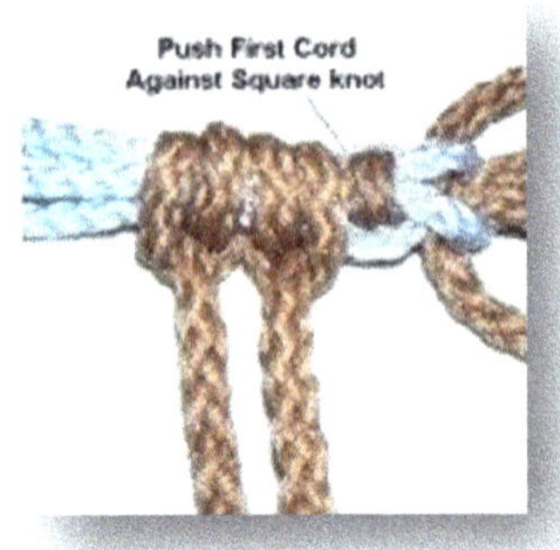

9. To make the Hammock Chair back side, tie 21 rows of Alternating Square Knots (ASK) to the 7-yard string. The starting row will contain the Step 5 mounting knots. The rest of the rows should be 1 "apart. If you want the back to be shorter in size you can reduce this. In row 1, tie LEFT Square Knot with 1-32 cords, and RIGHT SK with 33-64 cords. Redo for the odd numbered rows left (such as 3, 5, 7, etc.).In row 2, connect the LEFT Square Knot with 3-34 cords and RIGHT SK with 35-62 cords. Repeat the following even numbered rows cycle (4, 6, 8, etc.).
10. Then for the seat, strengthen the knots in row 22, so they lay 1/2 inch below those in row 21. Redo for remaining rows. If you like a tighter pattern, you should move the knots 1/4-inch apart, but make sure the panel is always stretched laterally. It is necessary to NOT tie the knots close together for the table. There must be at least some distance between rows or the panel is going to get too short. Stop when at least 23 rows have been joined (in this situation a minimum of 44 rows for both the back and the seat).
11. Hold the hammock chair with the support of the rings, if you haven't. Choose any two supporters from the LONG side (4.5-yard) that come from the right ring and two from the left ring. Diagonally transfer both of these cords into one another.It will be very much exactly what you did in step 3. From the Wrapped knot calculate at least 60 inches down. This is the location the cords are meant to touch. Tie the knot in the Square to briefly attach them. Place a seat

on top of those carrying cords, to check the Hammock Chair's size. The seat has to move up, because it's at a small angle to the chair's back. But it does not rise up too high or the Chair of the Hammock would not be comfortable. Change the seat where the holding cords are tied; this will make the seat shift upwards or downwards. Keep practicing for the Square knot organization, before you prefer the seat size.

12. When the lower cords have entered a suitable location, tightly tie the Square Knot. Use fabric glue while tightening the knot. This should hold the knot securely sealed.
13. Instead of letting them hang, move the edges of the new holding cords so two go to the right and the other two head to the left. Using Double Half Hitches to attach half the cords from seat to the right of the Square Knot, and the other half to the left. This is achieved exactly as in step 5; the only variation being the knot type used.Start in the center and move when you connect the cords (on both sides of SK) outwards. On the end of each cord tie a Barrel Knot, and it lies under the seat of the Hammock Chair, at the bottom edge. Finish the seat by choosing each of the two options: Trim the sides of the lines, but make sure that they are at least 2 inches long and move into the loops at the seat's BACK. Keep them in place using cement. Or you may cut the cords and leave a fringe, then mount them. At the bottom, attach a Barrel ties to avoid unraveling of the cords.
14. Arrange the cords left for helping the right hand into a pair of twos. You must start form the bottom and push up the top when you follow them to the back and sit on the right side. In row 42, the main side help is mounted right next to the SK, which at the right side.In row 42, the main side help is mounted right next to the SK, which at the yard) supports through the space next to the Square knot. Do the same for the other string, bring it into another spot; next to the same SK. make sure the supports at the side are vertical, with a little tension. Use an Overhand knot to tie the two strings together.Tighten the knots, and that meets the seat's Edge. Attach an extra Overhand knot next to the first one.

Making sure it stays at the back of the Hammock chair after securing this knot too.Pull the edges to the seat front before continuing to the next stage.

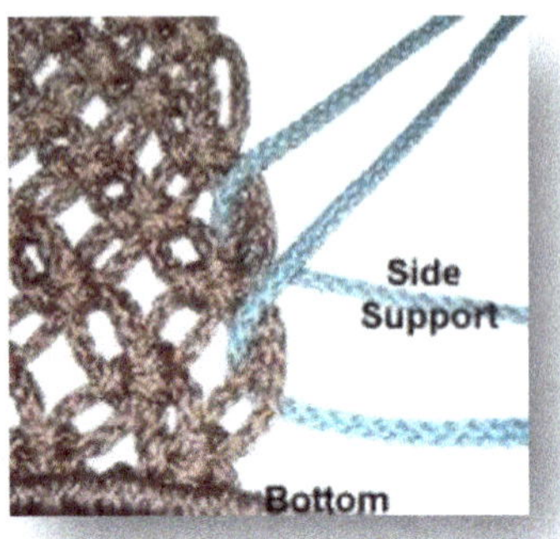

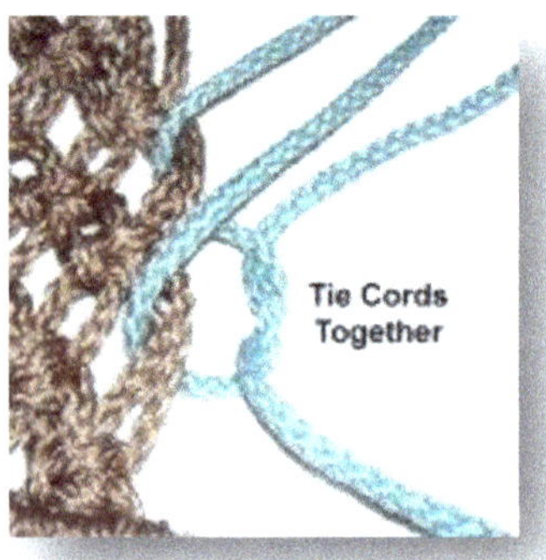

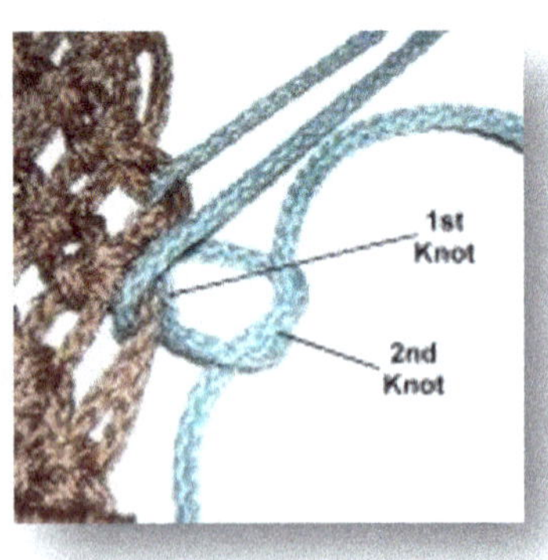

15. Redo step 11 with just the leftover LONG side supports, positioning them on the right side of the seat per 3rd section.And do the same for the Small side helps, while you operate in the upper field where Square Knot's rows are farther apart. There will also be room in between the supports per three sides. Ensure sure you place the supports as similar as possible to the Square Knots, even though the spaces are more important.

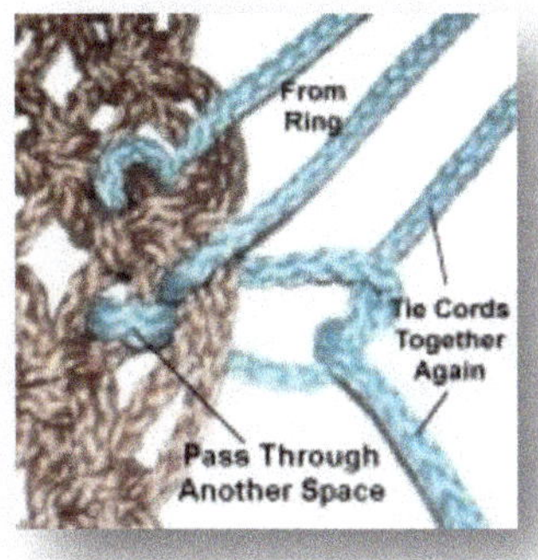

16. it's helpful to bring the support cords down the entire right side in place, then go back and tie them with the knots. This way, if appropriate, you may make improvements to their place.
17. Follow measures 11 and 12 through installing supports on the left foot. If required, make the appropriate changes to the ties, so the Hammock Chair hangs equally, before going on to the next stage.
18. Go back to where you began and move into another space the ends of the new side supports like before, to the left. Now attach the cords again, using 2 Overhand Knots (OK), as performed in stage no 11.Do this step for both sides on all sides on all other side supports current. Once finished, add the glue to the knots and allow it to dry before continuing.
19. To build a fringe using the remaining material from the side supports. OR you can use any extra ties to tie them to the table. Depending on your choice another alternative is to make Barrel knots at the end of both of the loose strings, so they rest near to the Square knots. Apply finishing glue then break off any excess content.

Chapter 7: Shopping Bag, Clutch Purse

This Clutch showcases picots with the sides of flap. A symmetrical stripe is created by using a 2nd color and switching between the right and left Square Knots. It is an extremely easy Macramé project, appropriate for a beginner. You must have some practice of tying Square Knots both left and right, but they are all explained as potion of the instructions. The dimensions of the finished clutch purse are 6.5 inches height (folded) and 9 inches wide. You can effortlessly create a broader version by adding more strings to it. Like the example illustrated, we are using two colors. A color is a brown, and B color is turquoise; you can use any color according to your preference.

Materials Needed:

- (50 yards) 4mm string material
- A small size button for the clasp
- Project board, some pins, glue, and tape

Knots Used:

- Barrel Knot (BK)
- Double Half Hitch (DHH)
- Alternating Square Knots (ASK)
- Square Knot (right and left both)

Preparation:

- Cut twenty cords of color A, each 4 yards in length.
- Cut extra strings into sets of two to keep the Clutch (striped) larger than 9 inches, make sure you have an even number of strands.
- Cut four cords of color B, each 4 yards in length.

Step by Step Instructions:

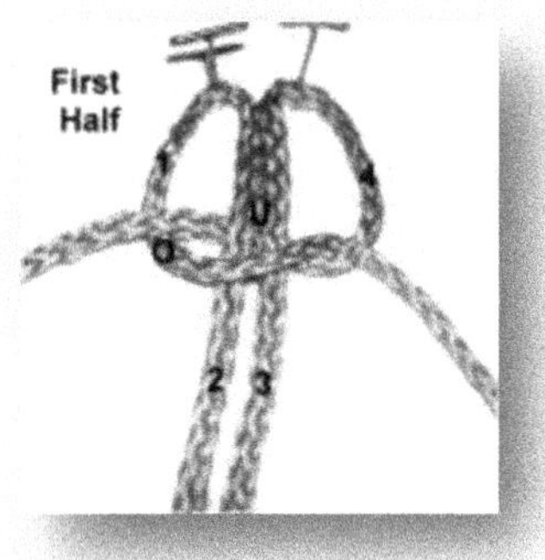

1. Fold in half two of A color cords and tie them in the middle. The following picture shows you how to wrap a (Left Square) Knot at the flap edge to form the picots. You can use these same set of details to produce all the left Square Knot used in creating the body of your Striped Clutch. Mentally mark the four parts, like they were four separate strings. For the left Square Knot, you always start by moving strand 1 towards the right, over filler cords 2 to 3 and under your working strand 4. Now move 4 cord to the left, under filler cords 2 to 3, and over the working string 1.Shift the knot's first half so that it sits half-inch below the fold (for half-inch picot). Cords 4 and 1 have changed places, and the position for the 2nd half of the SK is now reversed. Pull cord 1 towards the left, over strings 2 to 3, and underneath cord 4. Pull cord 4 towards the right, underneath cords 2 - 3, and over cord 1.

2. Revise 1 step with two cords in color B, making 1 picot loop design.
3. The following guidelines are for the right Knot (SK) picot designs. Create at least seven picots with A color design. If you want the clutch that is striped to be broader than nine inches, you can make more picots in this color.
4. Create one picot with B color at the top. For your right Square know, you begin by pulling 4 cord towards the left, over strings 2 to 3 and underneath strand 1. Now move strand 1 to the right, underneath strands 2 to 3, and over your working cord 4.

Move cord 4 to the right for the second half, over the filler cords 2-3 and underneath cord 1. Pull cord 1 towards the left, underneath cord 2-3, and over 4 cord.

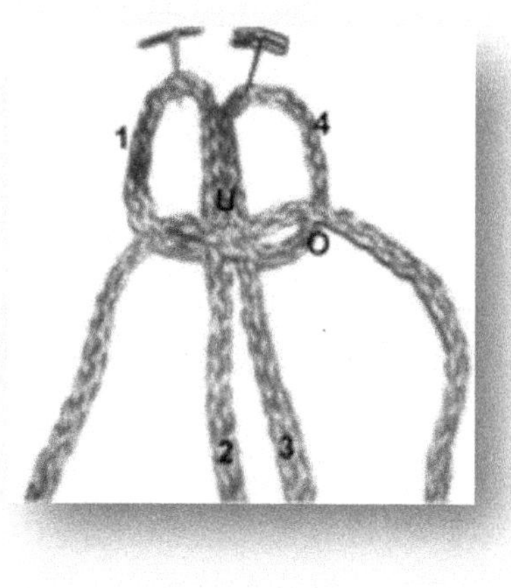

5. Organize on the board all picot designs as follows: Three A colors Left picots (from steps 1 to 2), followed by one B color Left picot design created in step 3. And one B color right picot created in step 4 that is follow by the 7 color A picot designs. Any other picot designs that you have created needs to be placed on the right side of others. The Clutch that is striped is created using (ASK) Alternating Square Knots. Before beginning, you must know how to switch cords, so if you do not know about how pattern of ASK work, then practice. For each row, you will begin from the left, so the directions make sense. Mentally number all the cords from 1 - 48. Pay very clear

focus on the direction of your Square Knot (left or right), as the stripe made with B color depends on the changes in direction. Left SK: The working cords on the left-hand side is moved first. Right SK: First, working cords moved will be on the right.

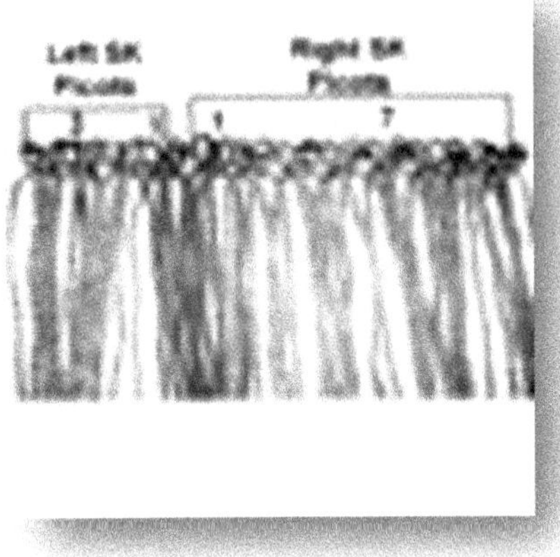

6. The 1st row is tied in groups of 4, starting with cord 3.The first 4 knots are left Square Knot made with the cords:
    - 3 - 6 of color A
    - 7 - 10 of color A
    - 11 – 14 of color B and A combined
    - 15 - 18 of color B

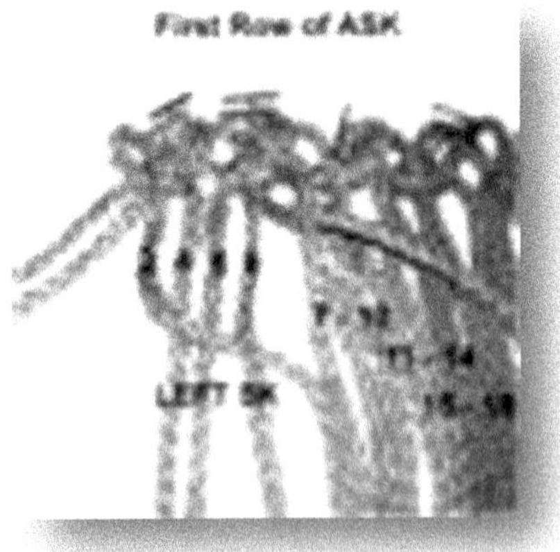

7. Now change to a right Square Knot when for which you are using cords 19 to 22,which is of the knots remaining Cords used are 27 43 46. color B and A combined. are all right Square Knots, of A color: 30, 23 26, 35 38, 31 34, 39 42, and

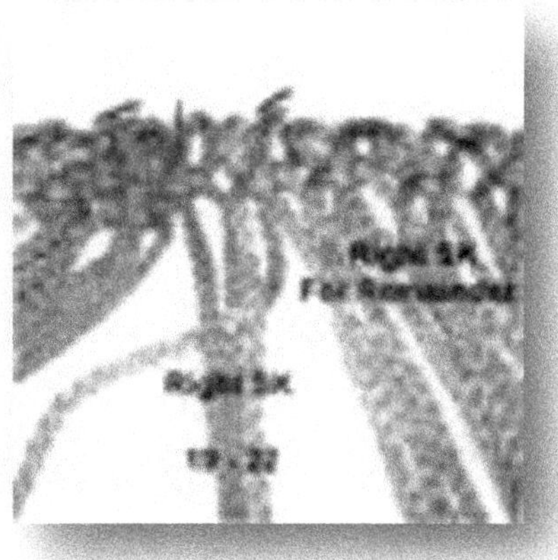

8. The 2nd of the row starts with the 4 remaining SK, tied with cords:
    - 1 - 4 (A color)
    - 5 - 8 (A color)
    - 9 - 12 (A color)
    - 13 - 16 (B color)

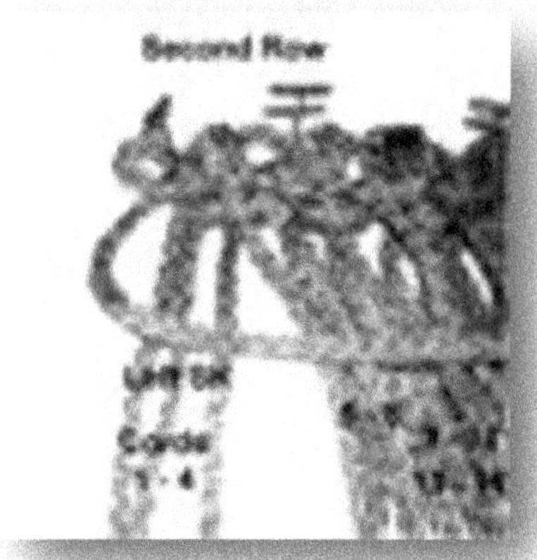

9. Tie the 1st right square knot with cords 17 to 20, of color B.The leftover loops are tied with the cords:

- 21 to 24,
- 25 to 28,
- 29, 32,
- 33 to 36,
- 37 to 40,
- 41 to 44,
- and 45 to 48.

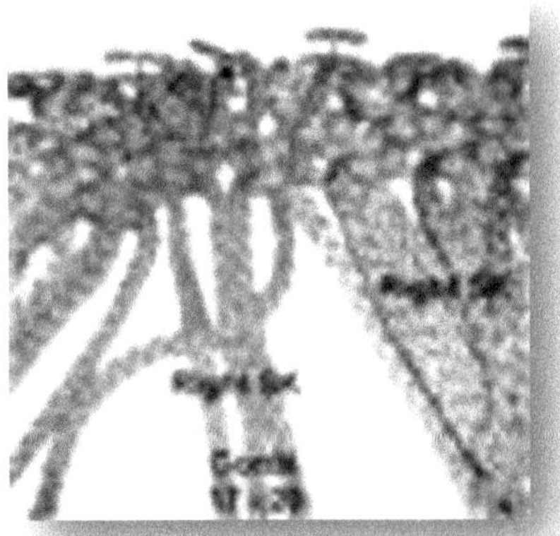

10. Redo 6th step but switch cords 2 & 3 before you do so. So, the first left Square Knot is created with cords 2-4-5-6. Cord 2 is required to be used as a cord working only one time, and this is good spot to do it. Repeat 7th step but switch cords 47 and 46 when you reach to the last ASK of that row. Now cords 43-44-45, and 47 will tie the final right Square Knot.

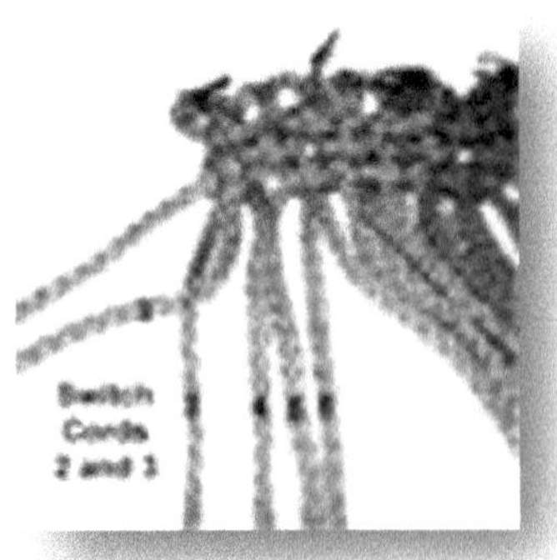

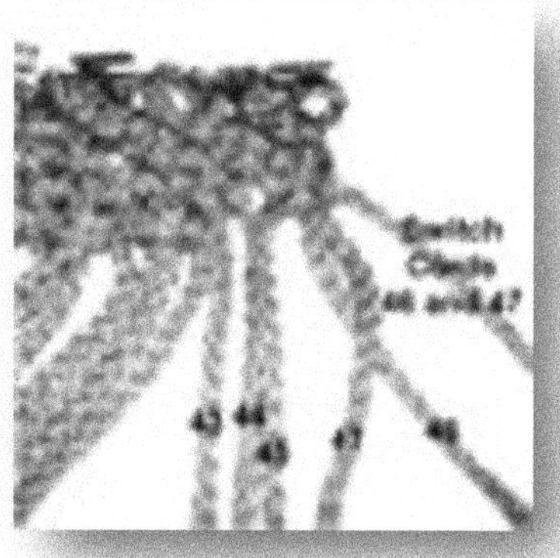

11. You repeat the steps 9 and 8 and then steps 7 and 6 for the rest of the striped clutch.
12. Repeat this step until the pattern is eighteen inches in length, from the top to the end row of ASK of the picots. Stop on the row where cords 3 to 46 are used (steps 7 and 6). **Useful tip:** Notice to make sure that the cords of color B are in the group always before starting each row. It is effortless to change cords around unintentionally, and That is BAD in this case. So be very careful while you are in the area that is striped and pay clear attention towards the cord position (see the picture for reference).The two colors are blended on a stripe in the rows where the steps repeat 7 and 6. The Square knot is always started with the color A thread. For this situation, that is chord 11 since you are tying a left Square Knot. In this row, the next blended color knot also begins with the same working cord of color A. That is string 22 in this situation since you are creating a right Square Knot. The last detail that you should observe is that the first 4 knots are all left Square Knots in each row, and the remainder are right SK's. Again, rightly changing directions at the right place is very important for creating this Striped Clutch. The lines will not be aligned otherwise.The Striped Clutch's front edge is made once all the ASK is attached or tied. Ensure that you have complete idea to tie a (DHH) Double Half Hitches.

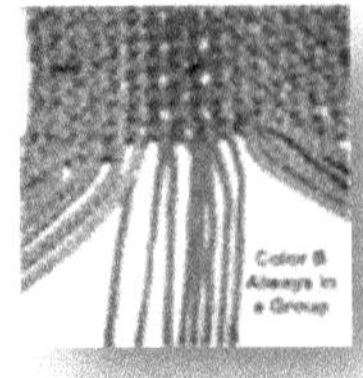

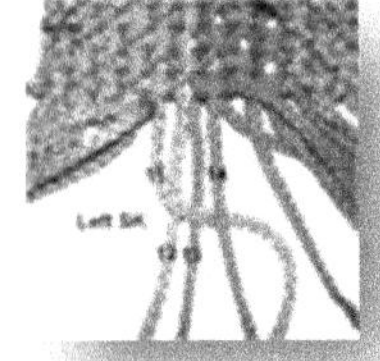

13. Pull 1 cord to the right, and so it lies on above of all other string.

14. This cord will work as a holding or stopping cord for the first row of DHH's.

15. Connect cords 2 to 47 with DHH knot to holding 1 cord. While creating each loop, rotating counterclockwise. Securely tie each knot. The formed bar should be placed against the last ASK row and bent a little to the right and left edges of the purse (just like in the next picture). When you move forwards, push the ties as tight as you can to one another, so that you have space for all the cords. Make sure that you do not connect cord 48 that is the last cord from the edge that is right to your Striped Clutch.

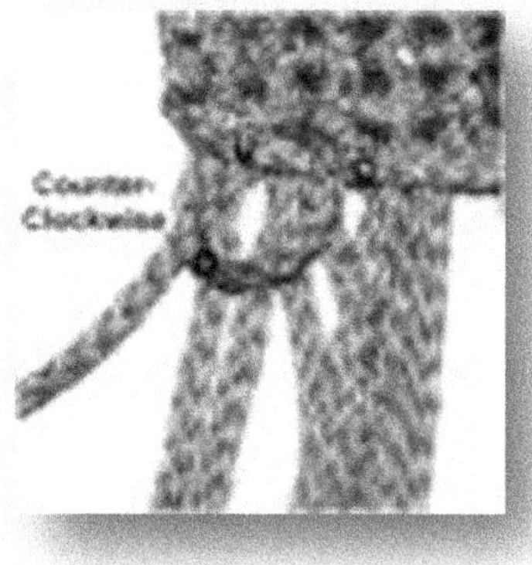

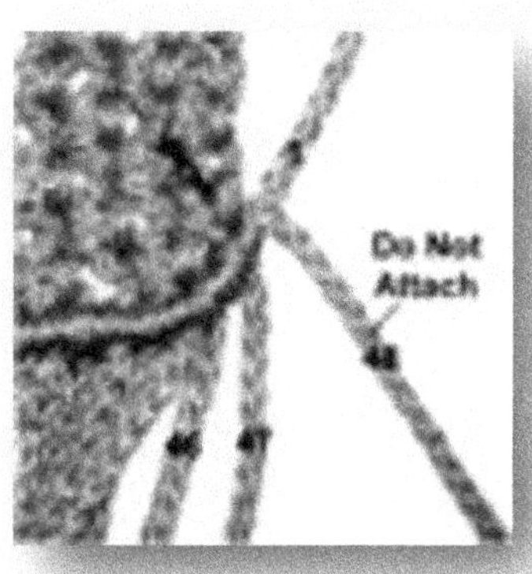

16. Now move cord 48 towards the left, located just below DHH's first section. Connect all the cords 47 to 2 in the same order with clockwise DHH knots. Once you got to the striped area, stop there.
17. End the strings by cutting them down to two inches each. Flip the clutch that is striped, so you are now working with the back. Slide single cord through the loop created under 1 row, which is the row underneath the ASK row. Use tweezers and pliers if needed for this step. This clutch must be lined, hiding the cut corners of the cords. If you do not want to do this, cut the cords a bit more, and add glue to stick them to the inside layer. You should burn (heat) the tips with a fire if using synthetic materials like nylon, to melt the substance at the edges to avoid the fray.

18. Now it is safe to lace the slides up to the clutch. Begin by taking measurement of the clutch down to five inches, starting from the picots. That is the flap of your clutch, so fold it here. Pull down 6 and half inches and again fold it. This will separate the back to the front end. The section with the DHH knots is your front. Grip the bag between your thighs or place it on one corner. There are knots in between the rows of Alternating Square Knot along the sides of the clutch. Line up the knots at the back and front sections so they are in direct to each other. There will be a single knot at the fold in the front and the back. Use two 18 "scrap cord pieces, or two new pieces, to tie the edges. Slip your lacing cord in the end rows of DHH's make sure you are as near to the edge as feasible from the front of the clutch. Now slide it straight across a loop from the back of the clutch.

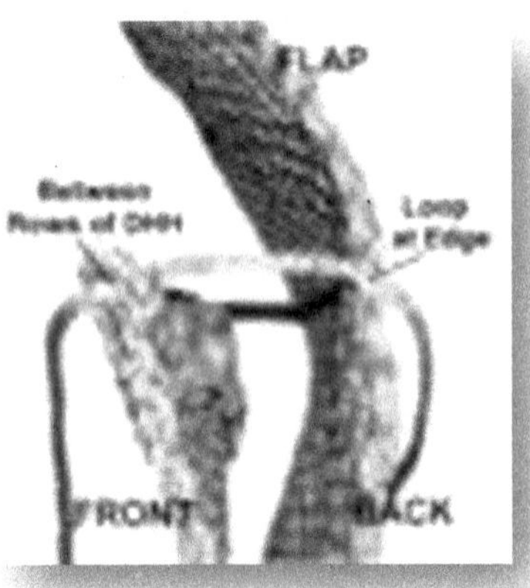

19. Make a cross using the two ends of your lacing cord's, and then move them into the loops of next set. Move them from in to outside.

20. Redo 18th step several times more, bypassing the ends from another loops, till you meet the flipped (folded) area in the front and the back. Once you reach the fold, move both your ends from the similar loop, bringing them to the inner side of your Striped Clutch. Before you go on, ensure the lacing is firm.

21. Turn the clutch inside out, so that the lacing string is on the outer side and easier to handle. Hold a Barrel Knot (Extra Loop and Overhand Knot) to hold it in place. Trim off the excess material near the knot, then add a little glue to it. When you are using a synthetic material cord, you can melt the material with the fire. Flip the clutch that is striped inside out, so that th

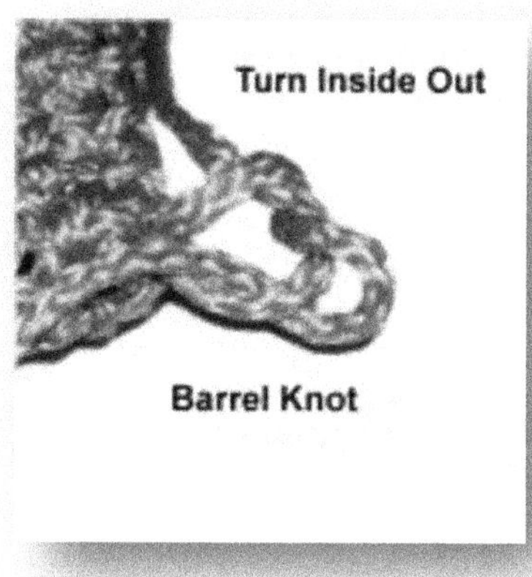

Chapter 8: Table Runner

All you need to know is three essential nodes, and you have a charming layer that works every season. If you know the knots learned here, you can tailor your table runner to the length of your table or change it totally and create a hanging macramé wall.

Supply: -12" wooden dowel –22 lengths of cotton rope measuring 3 mm –with cotton twine over the door–2" with dowel hanger scissors

- **Step 1:**

Apply cotton twine to each end of the dowel and hang it on the door hanger. Fold your first 16" rope strand in half and create a knot on your dowel. For even more thorough measures, see this article.

- **Step 2:**

Use the same beach to tie a second knot to the foundation line. This is regarded as a halving knot.

- **Step 3:**

Make sure they are clear and even.

- **Step 4:**

Repeat from the outside with the second, third and fourth ropes and tie another hitch-knot, so it is snug, etc. You're going to begin to see the trend. It's a half-hitch horizontal.

- **Step 5:**

Continue to tie successive cords throughout a single knot. You don't want to be so close that it's at the edges in the distance.

- **Step 6:**

From the right again, use the four outer strands to build a knot about 1.5" below the horizontal knots. See this macramé storage article for more information on a square knot. Out the four (five to eight) strands then tie another knot of nine to twelve strands. Keep skipping four before you cross the line.

- **Step 7:**

begin again on the right, use the four strands that you skipped (five to eight) and tie a square knot about 3" below the dowel.

- **Step 8:**

Continue tying four-strand sets in square knots until the row is ended. horizontal knots. Then use the following four strands to create another 1.5" square knot over the last square knot.

- **Step 9:**

Start as shown. You're not going to do anything with the last two lines.

- **Step 10:**

Going back from the right, build another series of half-hitch horizontal knot by repeating steps 3 through 7.

- **Step 11:**

From the left side, use the same base rope string and produce horizontal half-hitch of knots about 2.5" below. You're going to work on this from left to right.

- **Step 12:**

Starting from the left side, create a row of knots without skipping any threads that are roughly 1" below that line of knots. Instead, create a second row of the quadratic knot, miss the first two threads on the left, and tie a full line of quadratic knots. This is known as an alternating knot. You don't want much space between these rows so you can draw them closer together as each square node is inserted.

- **Step 13:**

Keep going until you have a total of approximately 13 rows of alternating knots. This segment is the core of your table runner so that everything else will represent what has already been woven above.

- **Step 14:**

Add another half-hitch horizontal knot from the outside left and work on the right.

- **Step 15:**

Downward nearly 2.5" and use the same base rope to create another horizontal half-hitch tie from the right to the right.

- **Step 16:**

Skip two outer strands of rope to the right for this segment and tie a square knot with strands three to six. Slip seven to 10 strands and use 11 to 14 strands to tie another knot. Repeat so that every four strands you missed. On the left, you're going to have six strands.

Turn one, and two rows left and tie three to six threads to a square knot around 1.5" underneath that last row of square knots. Then miss the four strands for the second row of square nodes and complete the sequence. This will leave you on the right side with six extra threads.

- **Step 17:**

Measure 11" from the last row of horizontal ties and tie a knot of the square by using the four outside strands to the right. Then tie the four in a square knot about 1.5" above the last knot.

Step 18: Repeat throughout.

Take note of how long the ends are on the other side as long as you like. Cut the twine of the cotton from your dowel and loosen all the knots of the lark carefully. Then cut the middle of the head of the lark and remove the sides.

You are now ready to set a charming table!

The middle of your dining table is the ideal place to put a centerpiece, so lie on a trivet, and you can find fresh flowers to anchor your hand. You can even use it as your giant cupboard in a breakfast bar, to make sure your kitchen looks best! You can also use the three common knots, the knot of the lark, the knot of half-hitch and the knot of the square to create a set of textured hanging walls!

Do you need something more colored? Use these stunning 3 mm and 5 mm Custom Macramé colored lines.

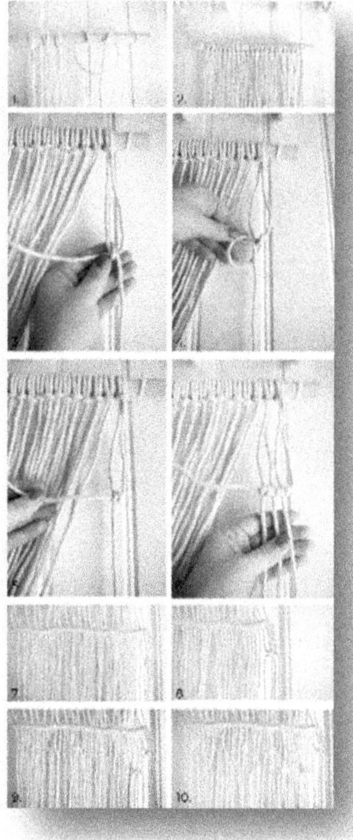

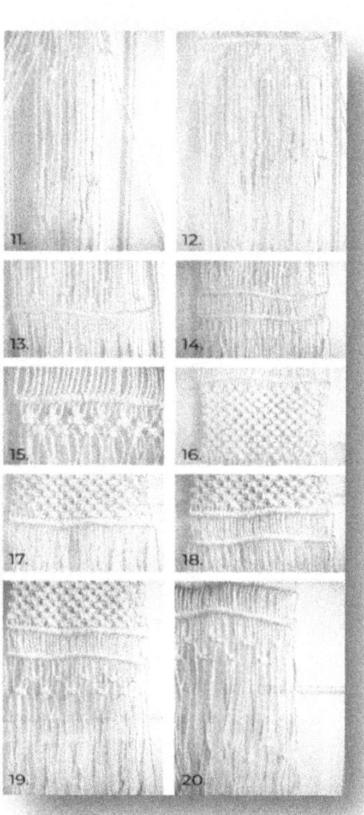

Chapter 9: Pillow Cover

Now we will learn how to create this beautiful DIY Macramé Pillow. It's not as complicated as it looks– the toughest part is to cut the long cords.

Knots used:

- Lark Head Knot
- Square Knot
- Double Half Hitch Knot

Materials Needed:

- Macramé Cord
- Sewing Machine/Thread (optional)
- Dowel or Stick
- Scissors
- Pillow cover and insert
- Tape Measure

Step by Step Instructions:

You can start with your pillow cover you have for this pillow, or create a simple pillow cover for any pillow available. Don't just make it yet-see first Stage no 5. In the illustration below, the pillow cover is made of drop fabric. This ended up exactly identical to the rope, which looks impressive.

However, if you do want to see the Macramé show, pick a different color for your pillow cover.

The cover in the picture is 20 x 20 inches, for reference. You have to ensure that your Macramé pattern can cover your pillow-but if not. The best news is if required, it can be stretched out.

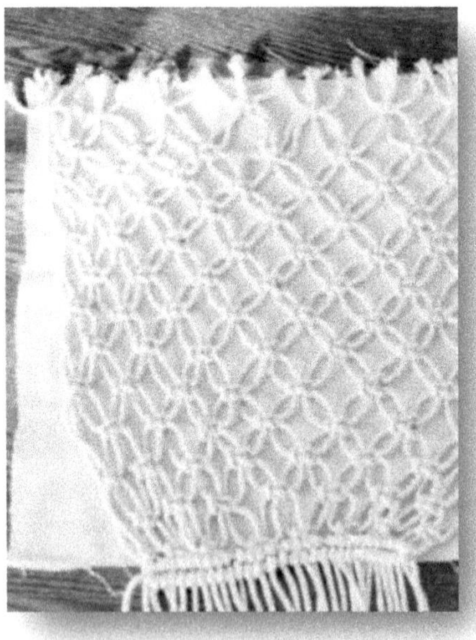

1. 12-foot string.
2. Using reverse lark's head knots tie all 16 cords to the dowel. You've learned how to tie a lark head knot to build the hat in the previous instructions.
3. For this cover, the pattern is the only rows of alternating square knots. Leave a little gap among each knot-around half of an inch as a reference. Having a little space makes the project run even quicker. You have to keep making the alternating square knots till you get down to the 20 " edge. Measure using the tape to watch where you are.Create two horizontal rows of (left-to-right, then right-to-left) double half hitch knots until you touch down the bottom.
4. So, now that we're done with the design cut off the excess from the bottom but keep a piece of the fringe – about 5 inches or

so. You may leave more or less, it's entirely up to you. So, you are either going to remove your pattern from the rod or just cut it off.

5. Break it off. Here's how you stick the Macramé design to your pillow. Before you stitch it up, whether you're making a cover by yourself – you're necessarily going to line up the design to the facade of the cover, leaving the cut edges a little over the top hang.

Place the back part over the cover, and Macramé design-right sides are facing each other-essentially you make a sandwich, and the Macramé design is called the "meat."

So, now patch your pillow cover's top edge-go above the cords too! Then it takes some degree of finesse, however you can fix it. Pin it all down to hold it all together.

Shove the Macramé pattern within your pillow to stitch rest of your pillow cover and stitch the remaining seams as usual.

Take another length of the Macramé cord and tie an easy knot on the back to attach the rest of the cover. Loop this string from out and in of square knots. Not only does this help spread out your pattern. Yet it must protect it down to the bottom too.

That is it! At the bottom edge of your pillow, the fringes will hang.
For A Ready Made Pillow Cover: You can open one of the joints and follow the instructions above or simply take the other piece of Macramé cord and thread it around the top. Then twist it backward. As mentioned above, you can also tie the sides.
Or, you could even hand stitch it to your pillow cover that certainly gives your sofa or easy chair a bit of an oomph. Yet this is sort of a novelty cushion – laying your head on it is kind of uncomfortable.

Chapter 10: Innovative and Modern Ways to Use Macramé in Your Home Décor

Macramé Home Décor

Now, it's time to learn how to make various home decors—simply by using the art of Macramé! Check them out and see which ones you want to make yourself!

Modern Macramé Hanging Planter

Plant hangers are really beautiful because they give your house or garden the feel of an airy, natural space. This one is perfect for condominiums or small apartments—and for those with minimalist, modern themes!

- Plant Pot
- 50 ft. Par cord (Parachute Cord)
- 16 to 20 mm wooden beads

First, fold in half 4 strands of the cord and then loop so you could form a knot.

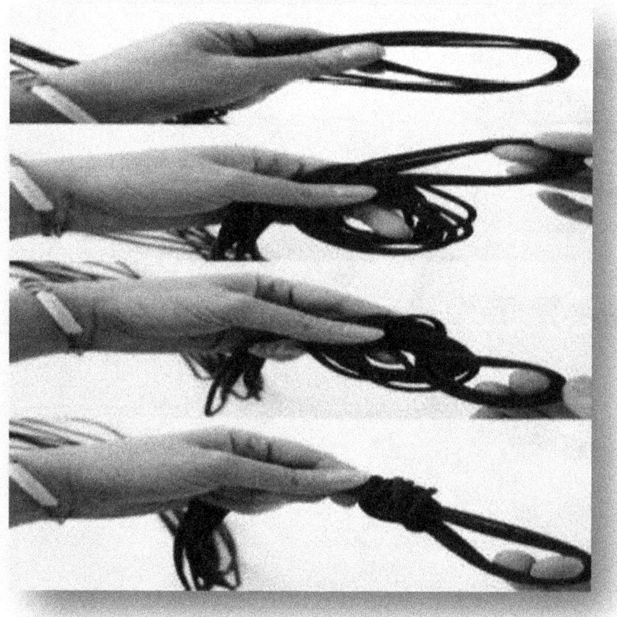

Now, divide the cords into groups of two and make sure to string 2 cords through one of the wooden beads you have on hand. String some more beads—at least 4 on each set of 2 grouped cords.

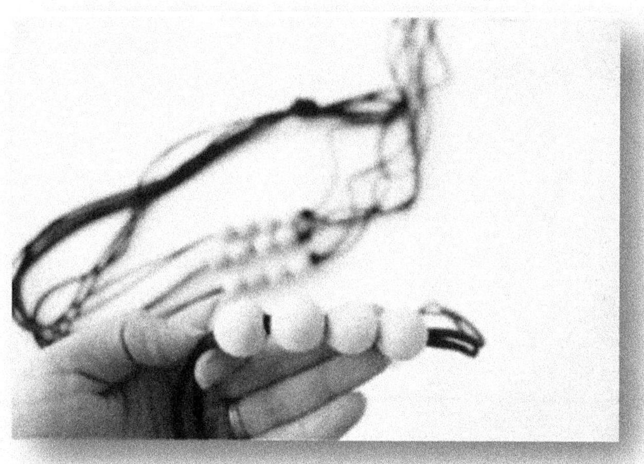

Then, measure every 27.5 inches and tie a knot at that point and repeat this process for every set of cords.

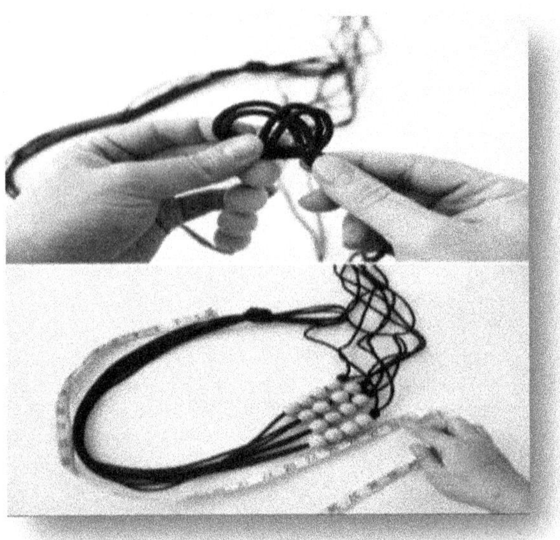

Look at the left set of the cord and tie it to the right string. Repeat on the four sets so that you could make at least 3" from the knot you have previously made.

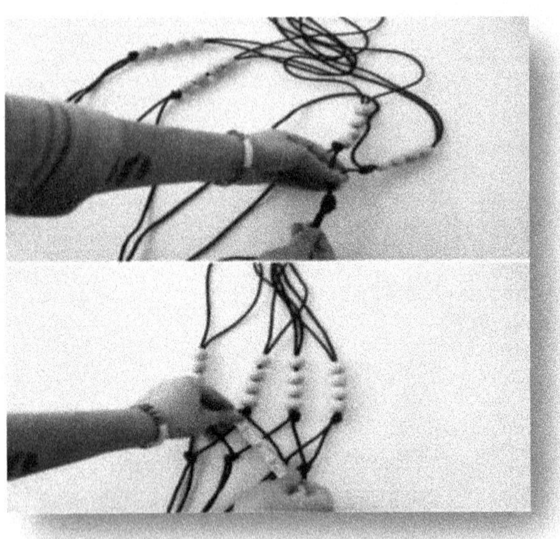

Tie another four knots from the previous knot that you have made. Make them at least 4.5" each.

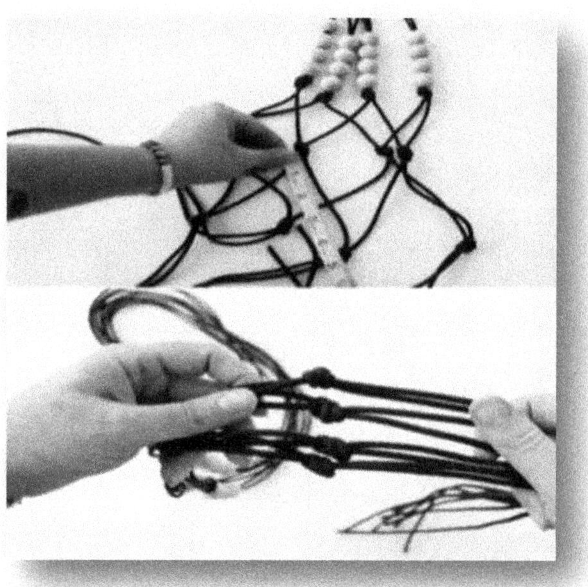

Group all of the cords together and tie a knot to finish the planter. You'll get something like the one shown below—and you could just add your very own planter to it!

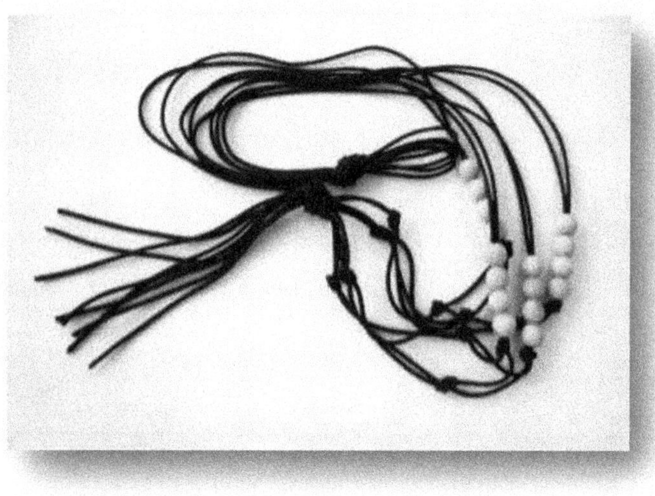

Mini Macramé Planters

Succulents are all the rage these days because they are just so cute and are really decorative! What's more is that you can make a lot of them and place them around the house—that will definitely give your place a unique look!

- Small container
- Garden soil/potting mix
- Succulents/miniature plants
- ¼ inch jump ring
- 8 yards embroidery thread or thin cord

Cut 36-inch of 8 lengths of cord. Make sure that 18 inches are already enough to cover enough half-hitches. If not, you can always add more. Let the thread loop over the ring and then tie a wrap knot that could hold all the cords together.

Create a half-twist knot by tying half of a square knot and repeating it multiple times with the rest of the cord.

Drop a quarter inch of the cord down and repeat step twice.

Arrange your planter and place it on the hanger that you have made.

Nail to the wall, and enjoy seeing your mini-planter!

Amazing Macramé Curtain

Macramé Curtains give your house the feel of that beach house look. You don't even have to add any trinkets or shells—but you can, if you want to. Anyway, here's a great Macramé Curtain that you can make!
Laundry rope (or any kind of rope/cord you want)

- Curtain rod
- Pins
- Lighter
- Tape

Tie four strands together and secure the top knots with pins so they could hold the structure down.

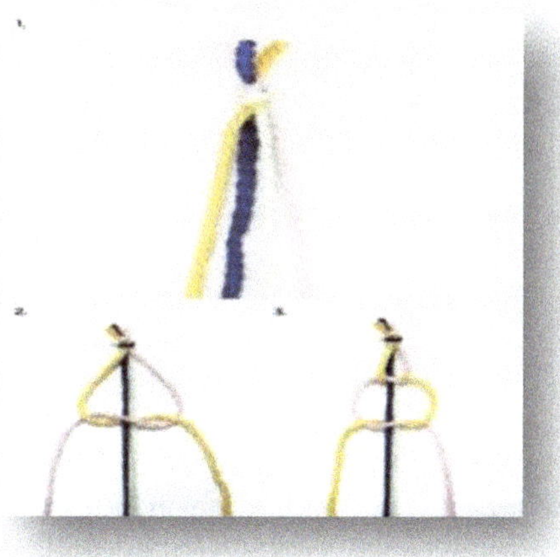

Take the strand on the outer right part and let it cross over to the left side by means of passing it through the middle. Tightly pull the strings together and reverse what you have done earlier.

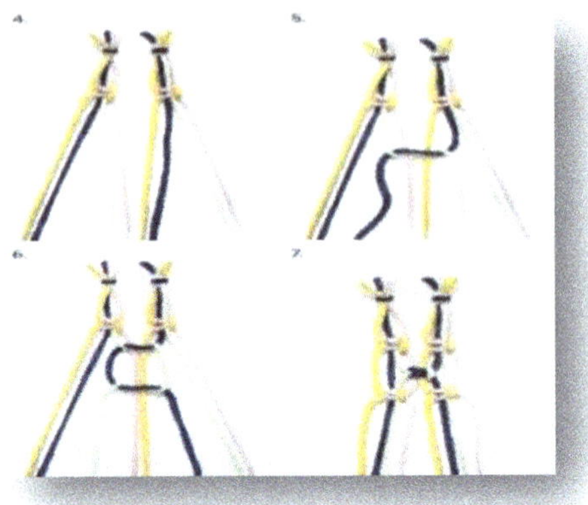

Repeat crossing the thread over four more times for the thread you now have in front of you. Take the strand on the outer left and let it pass through the middle, and then take the right and let it cross over the left side. Repeat as needed, then divide the group of strands to the left, and also to the right. Repeat until you reach the number of rows you want.

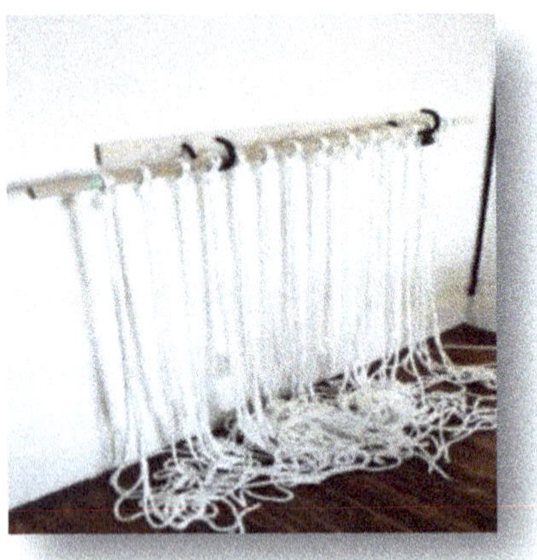

You can now apply this to the ropes. Gather the number or ropes you want—10 to 14 is okay, or whatever fits the rod, with good spacing. Start knotting at the top of the curtain until you reach your desired length. You can burn or tape the ends to prevent them from unraveling.

Braid the ropes together to give them that dreamy, beachside effect, just like what you see below.

That's it; you can now use your new curtain!

Macramé Wall Art

Adding a bit of Macramé to your walls is always fun because it livens up the space without making it cramped—or too overwhelming for your taste. It also looks beautiful without being too complicated to make. You can check it out below!

- Large wooden beads
- Acrylic paint
- Painter's tape
- Paintbrush
- Wooden dowel
- 70 yards rope

Attach the dowel to a wall. It's best to just use removable hooks so you won't have to drill anymore.

Cut the rope into 14 x 4 pieces, as well as 2 x 5 pieces. Use 5-yard pieces to bookend the dowel with. Continue doing this with the rest of the rope.

Then, start making double half-hitch knots and continue all the way through, like what's shown below.

Once you get to the end of the dowel, tie the knots diagonally so that they wouldn't fall down or unravel in any way. You can also add the wooden beads any way you want, so you'd get the kind of décor that you need. Make sure to tie the knots after doing so.

Use four ropes to make switch knots and keep the décor all the more secure. Tie around 8 of these.

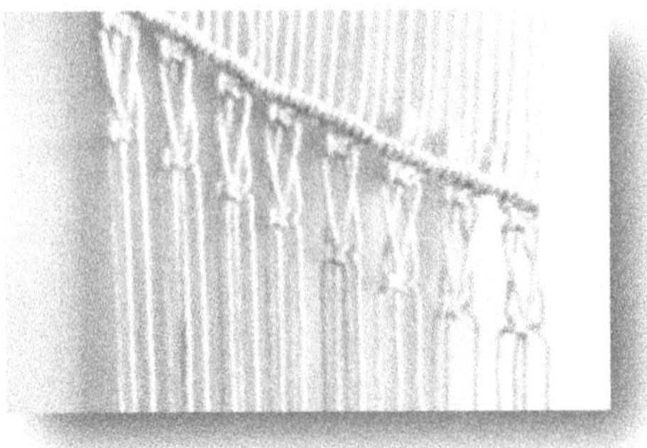

Add a double half hitch and then tie them diagonally once again.

Add more beads and then trim the ends of the rope.

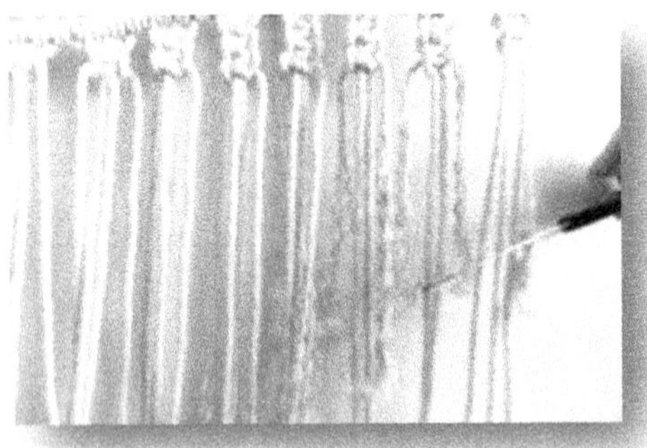

Once you have trimmed the rope, go ahead and add some paint to it. Summery or neon colors would be good.

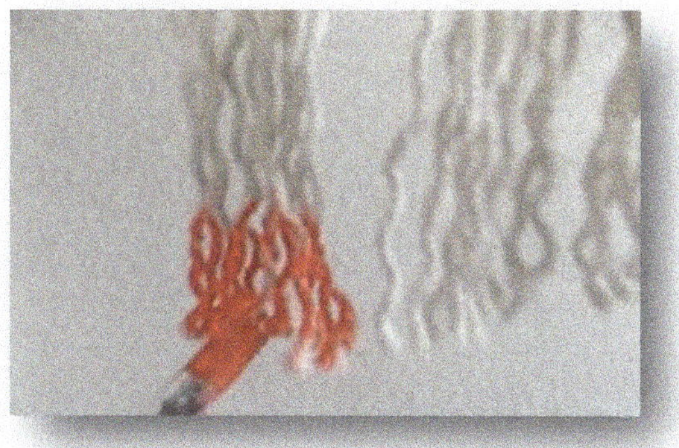

That's it! You now have your own Macramé Wall Art!

Hanging Macramé Vase

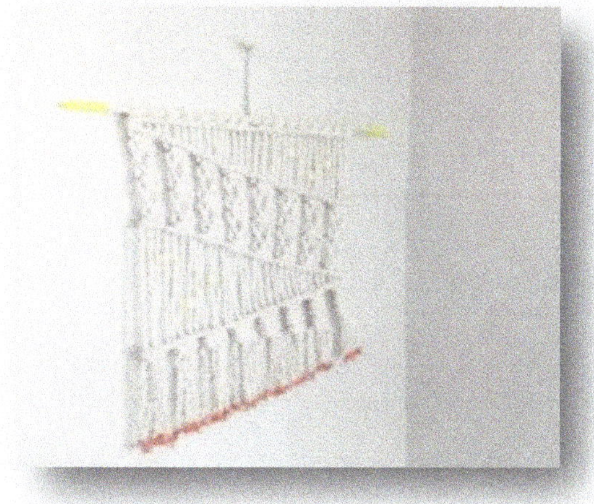

To add a dainty, elegant touch to your house, you could create a Macramé Vase. With this one, you'll have to make use of basket stitches/knots—which you'll learn about below. It's also perfect for those who really love flowers—and want to add a touch of nature at home!

- Masking tape
- Tape measure or ruler
- 30 meters thick nylon cord
- Small round vase (with around 20 cm diameter)

Cut eight cords measuring 3.5 yards or 3.2 meters each and set aside one of them. Cut a cord that measures 31.5 inches and set it aside, as well. Then, cut one cord that measures 55 inches.

Now, group eight lengths of cord together—the ones you didn't set aside, of course, and mark the center with a piece of tape.
Wrap the cords by holding them down together and take around 80 cm of it to make a tail—just like what you see below.

Wrap the cord around the back of the long section and make sure to keep your thumb on the tail. Then, wrap the cord around the main cord group. Make sure it is firm, but don't make it too tight. If you can make the loop bigger, that would be good, too.

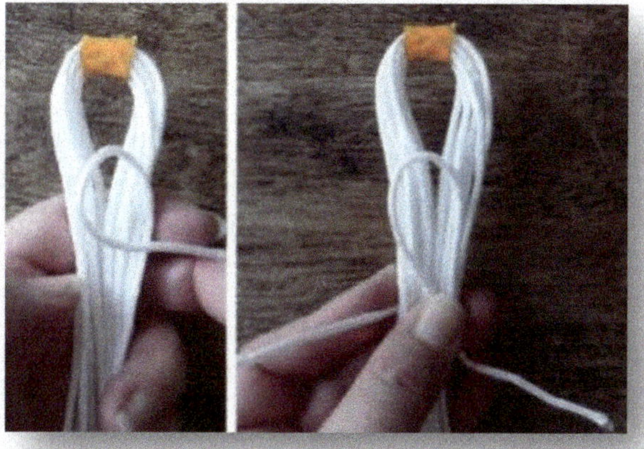

Do it 13 more times through the loop and go and pull the tail down so the loop could soften up. Stop letting the cords overlap by pulling them whenever necessary and then cut both ends so they would not be seen anymore.

Divide the cords into groups of four and secure the ends with tape.

Get the group of cords that you have not used yet and make sure to measure 11.5 inches from the beginning—or on top. Do the overhand knot and get the cord on the left-hand side. Fold it over two of the cords and let it go under the cord on the right-hand side.

Fold the fourth cord and let it pass under the leftmost cord then up the loop of the first cord. Make sure to push it under the large knot so that it would be really firm.

Make more half-hitches until you form more twists. Stop when you see that you have made around 12 of them and then repeat with the rest of the cords.

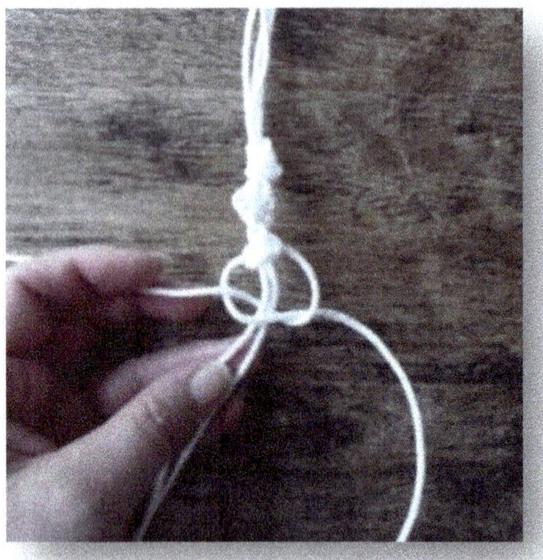

Now, it's time to make the basket for the vase. What you have to do here is measure 9 centimeters from your group of cords. Tie an overhand knot and make sure to mark with tape.

Let the two cord groups come together by laying them side by side.

Tie the cords down but make sure to keep them flat. Make sure that the knots won't overlap, or else you'd have a messy project—which isn't what you'd want to happen. Use two cords from the left as starting point and then bring the two cords on the right over the top of the loop. Loop them together under the bottom cords and then work them back up once more.

Now, find your original loop and thread the same cords behind them. Then, let them pass through the left-hand cords by making use of the loop once more.

Let the knot move once you already have it in position. It should be around 3 inches or 7.5 cm from the overhand knots. After doing so, make sure that you flatten the cords and let them sit next to each other until you have a firm knot on top. Keep dividing and letting cords come together.

Next, get the cord on the left-hand side and let it go over the 2nd and 3rd cords before folding the fourth one under the first two cords. You'd then see a square knot forming between the 2nd and 3rd cords. You should then repeat the process on the right-hand side. Open the cord on the right side and let it go under the left-hand cord. Repeat this process thrice, then join the four-square knots that you have made by laying them out on a table.

You'll then see that the cords have come together at the base. Now, you have to start wrapping the base by wrapping a 1.4 meter cord and wrap around 18 times.

To finish, just cut the cords the way you want. It's okay if they're not of the same length so that there'd be variety—and they'd look prettier on your wall. Make sure to tie overhand knots at the end of each of them before placing the vase inside.

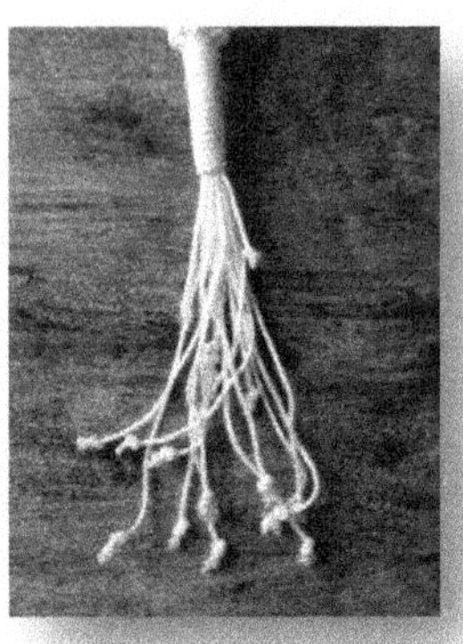

Enjoy your new hanging vase!

Chapter 11: Pizzaz Anklet

This pattern seemed to write itself as an uncomplicated, fun piece. The use of multiple cord colors keeps it cheery while offering many design choices. For ease of use it has a button closure. The pattern creates a 10 inch anklet… just repeat the pattern to enlarge, but remember to cut your cord a bit longer than specified.

Knots Used: Vertical Lark's Head Knot**,**Flat Knot (aka square knot) Double,Double Half Hitch Knot

Supplies:

- C-Lon cord, 5 ft 6 in., Rose (x1), Mint (x1), Apricot (x1)
- 5mm button bead (x1)
- Light green size 11 seed beads (x108)
- Pink size 11 seed beads (x64)
- Light pink size 6 seed beads (x40)
- Beacon 527 glue

Instructions:

1. Place all 3 cords together and find the center. Tie a loose overhand knot at the center point and place the cords on your project board as shown with the green on the left and the pink on the right:
2. Using the outer most cord on each side, tie about 10 flat knots around the inner cords. Untie the overhand knot and place the flat knots in a horseshoe shape. Pin the ends in place and check to see if your button bead will fit (snugly) through the opening. Adjust flat knots as necessary.

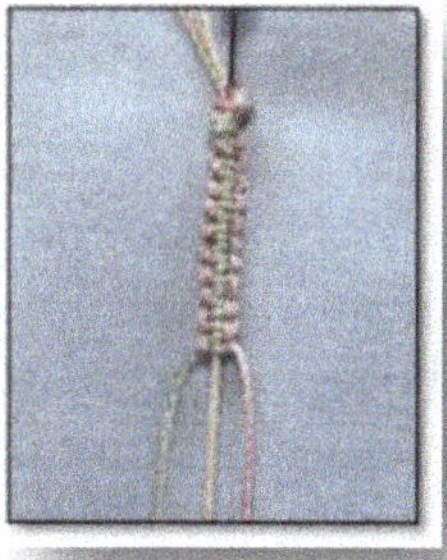

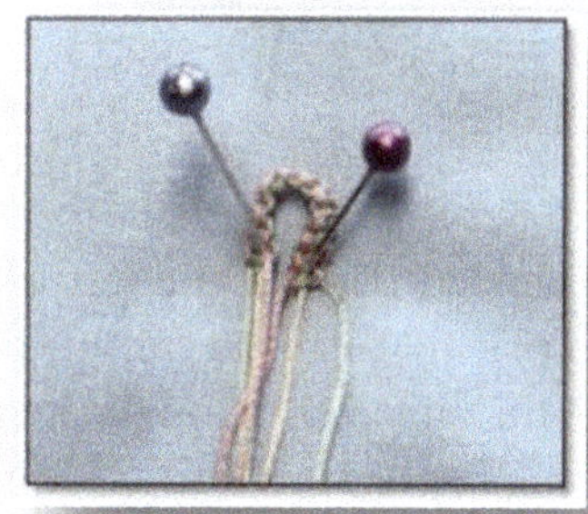

3. Rearrange the cords so that both green cords are on the left, the apricot cords are in the center and both pink cords are on the right. Using the outer cord on each side (green and a pink) tie a flat knot.

4. Separate the cords 2-2-2. Find the second cord in from each side and thread on 3 size 11 light green seed beads.

5. Take the left apricot cord and tie a VLH knot onto the beaded cord to the left of it. Tug gently on the apricot cord to form an arc. Now take the right apricot cord and thread it through the arc, then tie a VLH knot onto the beaded cord to the right. Tug gently on the apricot cord to form an arc.

6. Find the left cord (green) and attach it to the beaded green cord with a VLH knot. Tug gently to create an arc to the outside. Repeat with the right cord (pink onto pink).

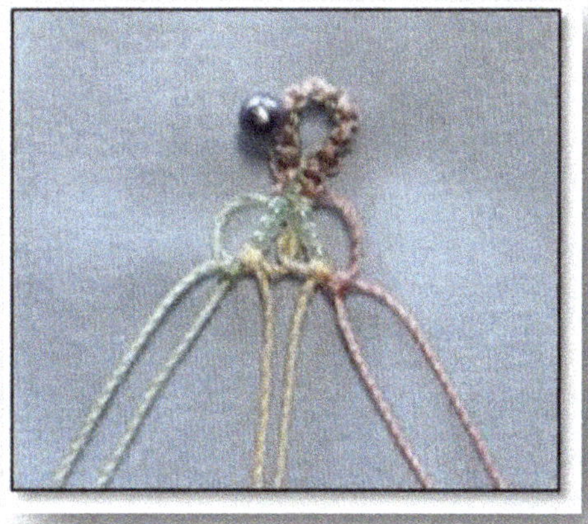

7. Repeat steps 4-6, then tie a flat knot with the outer cord on each side. Note: As you go on, if the left green cord is getting too short, swap it with the longer green cord next to it either before or after this flat knot.

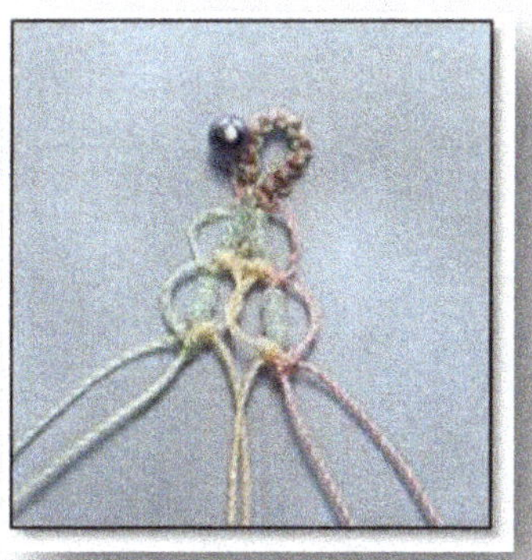

8. Take the left cord and thread on four size 11 pink seed beads, one size 6 pale pink seed bead and another four size 11 pink seed beads, then set it aside. Find the right cord (pink) and place it to the left, over the other 4 cords, as the holding cord (HC). Tie diagonal double half hitch (DDHH) knots onto it from right to left.

9. Find the right cord and thread onto it three pale pink size 6 beads. Skip the next cord in and place on the next cord a size 6 pale pink bead.

10. Take the HC from the left and place it to the right. Tie DDHH knots onto it from left to right. Retrieve the set aside cord and use it along with the far right cord to tie a flat knot around the other cords.Repeat steps 4 through 10 until you have reached 9 1/2 inches. With the center 2 cords, thread 2 or 4 cords through the button bead. Use the remaining cords to tie a flat knot

around it. Glue the back of the flat knot and let dry. Then trim the cords and glue once more.

For this one I used Teal, Blue Lagoon and Amethyst cord:

Conclusion

This book is written in honor of your spirit, to delve into the experience of Macramé despite its lack of demand. A tiny community around the globe still practice macramé. Most of these people are mature and older and may have learned the art of Macramé during its heyday in the '70s.

Macramé has been embraced as a versatile, potential, trendy craft worthy of complementing other fashionable products for the expansion in the process of product development, which has a culture and economic interests as well as a sustaining culture. Some of the assumptions that have been drawn are that macramé craft has become a whole feature of our traditional arts, especially among the youth, and is still experiencing increasingly notable change.

Now the art of Macramé is reviving. Because of its use in jewelry that has been making the rounds in the fashion industry. The same decorative patterns are seen in elegant clothes, purses, caps, and belts.

Macramé is a way to create textiles that use knots rather than other techniques of weaving or knitting. Macramé was initially used by sailors to decorate artifacts or their ships, but now it is often used to make shoes, containers, sheets, hangers for plants, and other things like wall hangings for walls.

In Victorian era, Macramé was remarkably popular as a lacework and was used for decorations on everything from jackets to underclothing, curtains, ornaments and jewelry. During the 70's it made another comeback, using the kind of jute plant holders and Macramé bird wall hangers.

Macramé has become popular once again, and today is seen in the form of Macramé jewelry, clothing, and accessories. If you are learning how to Macramé or you've been at it for years, you will find lots of great information.

In this book you have learned some common knots, patterns, and methods used in macramé instructions for creating different designs or patterns. You have also learned about the different kinds of materials used for macramé. There are several recognized fabrics used to do macramé. These include silk, rayon, raffia threads, shoe sewing threads, cotton threads, jute, cloth strips, leather strips, shoelace, and all other lightweights, malleable, foldable, and durable and hand safe fabrics.

Yet jute, silk, linen, and cotton are the most common fabrics used for Macramé as they tie easily, come in several sizes, can be dyed, and are readily available. Leather and suede are also sometimes used for macramé.

You have also learned about a wide variety of knots and knots combinations that are found in macramé, including the square knot, a half knot, half hitch, and the larks head knot. You can learn various patterns which can be created depending on the knots used and ether they are used individually or in addition to others. Some ordinary bags, and also the friendship bracelets created by many kids, are made with macramé as well.

This book has featured a vied range of patterns ranging from essential pieces like decorative ornaments and key chains to more complex ones like bags, jewelries, and planters. This book is an excellent guide for both fresher and experienced Macramé Lovers. I hope you have learned something.

CPSIA information can be obtained
at www.ICGtesting.com
Printed in the USA
BVHW011207100221
599800BV00005B/268